breakfast comforts

ENTICING RECIPES
FOR THE MORNING

RICK RODGERS

PHOTOGRAPHS
MAREN CARUSO

weldon**owen**

CONTENTS

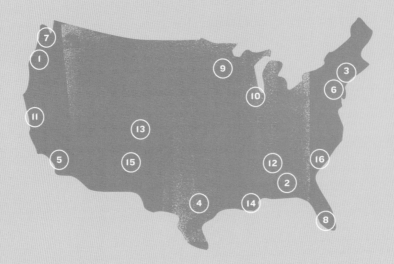

OUR FAVORITE
BREAKFAST RESTAURANTS
around the country

1 DAILY CAFE PORTLAND, OR
WHOLE WHEAT PANCAKES WITH
STRAWBERRY-RHUBARB
COMPOTE ★ 21

2 HIGHLAND BAKERY ATLANTA, GA
SWEET POTATO PANCAKES
WITH PECANS AND BROWN-SUGAR
SAUCE ★ 31

3 SARABETH'S NEW YORK, NY
SWEET CHEESE–STUFFED BLINTZES
WITH HONEYED BLUEBERRIES ★ 41

4 KERBEY LANE CAFE AUSTIN, TX
TEXAS-STYLE MIGAS WITH
RANCHERO SAUCE ★ 52

5 BLU JAM CAFE LOS ANGELES, CA
BREAKFAST QUESADILLAS
WITH CHICKEN, SPINACH,
AND AVOCADO ★ 62

6 JACK'S FIREHOUSE
PHILADELPHIA, PA
PHILLY CHEESESTEAK OMELET WITH
ONIONS AND BELL PEPPERS ★ 77

7 PORTAGE BAY CAFE SEATTLE, WA
CRAB CAKE EGGS BENEDICT
WITH SAUTÉED SPINACH ★ 87

**8 MICHAEL'S GENUINE FOOD
AND DRINK** MIAMI, FL
WHITE CHOCOLATE SCONES
WITH MEYER LEMON CURD ★ 105

9 HELL'S KITCHEN MINNEAPOLIS, MN
STICKY-SWEET PECAN
CARAMEL ROLLS ★ 116

10 HOTCHOCOLATE CHICAGO, IL
MONKEY BREAD WITH STRAWBERRY
CARAMEL SAUCE ★ 129

11 UNIVERSAL CAFE
SAN FRANCISCO, CA
BREAKFAST FLATBREAD WITH
PROSCIUTTO AND TOMATO ★ 146

12 SWEET 16TH - A BAKERY
NASHVILLE, TN
"GRITTATA" BREAKFAST
CASSEROLE ★ 155

13 SNOOZE, AN A.M. EATERY
DENVER, CO
CORNED BEEF HASH WITH
CARAMELIZED ONIONS AND
CHILES ★ 163

14 THE RUBY SLIPPER CAFE
NEW ORLEANS, LA
NEW ORLEANS–STYLE BBQ SHRIMP
AND GRITS ★ 170

15 CAFE PASQUAL'S SANTA FE, NM
PAPAS FRITAS WITH SANTA FE–
STYLE CHILE SAUCE ★ 180

16 HOMINY GRILL CHARLESTON, SC
HIGH-RISE BISCUITS WITH
SAUSAGE GRAVY ★ 192

HOMINY GRILL

JACK'S

Jack's

UNIVERSAL cafe

fresh simple pure

MICHAEL'S

GENUINE

FOOD & DRINK

Est. 2006

miami design district

d

Feather-light pancakes dripping with maple syrup; fluffy cinnamon rolls still warm from the oven; farm-fresh eggs with crisp peppered bacon and golden hashbrowns: these mouthwatering icons of the breakfast table are meant for slow-paced mornings, when you can relax and enjoy your meal over a strong cup of coffee and unhurried conversation.

Breakfast was the first meal that I learned to make by myself, so it holds a unique place in my culinary training. My parents taught me how to make French toast first. I clearly remember standing on a chair in front of the stove with a bowl of custard, a stack of bread, and a hot griddle at the ready. Next I learned to make pancakes and waffles, and then soft scrambled eggs and crisp fried bacon; before long, I had a fairly extensive breakfast repertoire. One of my fondest childhood memories is of my brothers and me helping cook a big weekend breakfast for the family, taking turns at the griddle to keep up with the demand for flapjacks.

I went on to become a professional cook, and my breakfast-making skills were put to the test when I got a job at a popular restaurant famous for its egg dishes. The kitchen went through hundreds of eggs every breakfast shift, and though it was hectic on busy weekend mornings, I loved my job. Making the first meal of the day for someone carries a certain responsibility, because the success of the meal can affect that person's entire day.

Breakfast Comforts celebrates the morning meal as a time to renew and replenish with satisfying, tasty food and good company. A comforting breakfast at home can be a quiet, intimate meal with your significant other, or a lively brunch with friends and family. It can also be spent alone, still in your robe and slippers, savoring a favorite dish, bite by bite, while slowly flipping through the newspaper. Whatever the situation, these recipes are the very best, most scrumptious versions of beloved dishes that are as familiar as they are nourishing.

I've also included specialties from eighteen carefully chosen restaurants from around the country that are renowned for their exceptional breakfasts, concentrating on neighborhood places and dishes that reflect the local cuisine. These restaurants truly represent the spirit of great breakfast dining, and pride themselves on freshly made food, served with a smile. Their offerings include such lip-smacking pastries as gooey cinnamon-pecan rolls (based on a restaurant owner's family recipe), and more hearty fare, like the crab-cake eggs Benedict, a classic brunch dish with a Seattle twist.

The recipes begin with a chapter devoted to the griddle cakes that are uniquely breakfast fare, including pancakes, waffles, and French toast. These are followed by a large collection of egg recipes that runs the gamut from traditional and mild-mannered (quiches, omelets, and baked eggs) to colorful and spicy (burritos, tacos, and chilaquiles), and everything in between. Next, recipes for the sweet treats that no one can resist, including tender apricot-ginger muffins, blackberry-laden cinnamon coffeecake, and even a few homemade doughnuts, all perfect for indulging with a steaming cup of coffee or tea. In the Savory Delights chapter, you'll find main dishes that are not necessarily egg-centric, such as a tomato-and-prosciutto breakfast flatbread and a variety of potato hashes. The selection is rounded out with the side dishes and accompaniments that we crave at breakfast time, with recipes for maple-glazed bacon, flaky biscuits (equally sublime with or without sausage gravy), and hash-browned potatoes. At the end of the book, there is a selection of favorite breakfast drinks, both hot and cold, to accompany your meal.

In our busy world, mornings can become an exercise in rushing, and all too often breakfast is a meal that is grabbed on the run. But it is important to set aside some time to truly enjoy the first hours of the day with a meal that makes you feel good. The appetizing recipes in this book are designed to inspire you to do so.

Rick Rodgers

FROM THE GRIDDLE

ALMOND-CRUSTED
FRENCH TOAST WITH BERRIES

6 large eggs

1 cup (8 fl oz/250 ml)
half-and-half

2 tablespoons sugar

Finely grated zest
of 1 orange

¾ teaspoon almond
extract (optional)

½ teaspoon
pure vanilla extract

8 thick slices challah
or other egg bread,
preferably day-old

Canola oil or
Clarified Butter
(page 212) for cooking

1 cup (4 oz/125 g)
sliced almonds

1 cup (4 oz/125 g)
raspberries

Pure maple syrup
for serving

MAKES 4 SERVINGS

Challah is my bread of choice here because it really absorbs the custard, creating an eggy, sweet version of French toast similar to the *pain perdu* of New Orleans. Crunchy almonds, fresh raspberries, and fragrant orange zest bring this classic breakfast dish to a whole new level.

◇◇

1 Preheat the oven to 350°F (180°C). Have ready 2 rimmed baking sheets. In a large shallow bowl, whisk together the eggs, half-and-half, sugar, orange zest, almond extract, if using, and vanilla. Add the bread to the egg mixture and turn gently to coat evenly. Let stand until the bread has soaked up some of the egg mixture, about 1 minute.

2 Place a griddle over medium heat until hot. Lightly oil the griddle and one of the baking sheets. Spread the almonds on a plate. One piece at a time, remove the bread from the egg mixture, letting the excess liquid drip back into the bowl. Dip one side of the bread into the almonds, pressing gently to help the nuts adhere. Place on the ungreased baking sheet. Repeat with the remaining bread slices.

3 Place the bread slices on the griddle, almond side down, and cook until the nuts begin to brown, about 2 minutes. Flip and cook the other sides until golden brown, about 2 minutes more. Transfer to the greased baking sheet, almond side down, and bake until the center of the bread is heated through but still moist, about 10 minutes.

4 Serve the French toast piping hot, almond side up, topped with a handful of raspberries and drizzled with maple syrup.

CHEESE-AND-MARMALADE
FRENCH TOAST SANDWICHES

4 large eggs

1 cup (8 fl oz/250 ml) whole milk

Finely grated zest of 1 orange

2 tablespoons fresh orange juice or orange-flavored liqueur

½ teaspoon pure vanilla extract

8 thick slices challah or other egg bread

½ cup (4 oz/125 g) whipped cream cheese, at room temperature

6 tablespoons orange marmalade

Canola oil or Clarified Butter (page 212) for cooking

Unsalted butter, at room temperature, for serving

Pure maple syrup for serving

MAKES 4 SERVINGS

For those of us who grew up eating plain French toast made from generic white bread, this decadent stacked version filled with cream cheese and marmalade is a revelation. To ensure the sandwiches cook through, I like to brown them on the griddle and then pop them in the oven to finish.

1 Preheat the oven to 350°F (180°C). Have ready a rimmed baking sheet. In a large shallow bowl, whisk together the eggs, milk, orange zest and juice, and vanilla. Lay 1 bread slice on a work surface and spread with one-fourth each of the cream cheese and marmalade. Top with another slice. Repeat with the remaining bread, cream cheese, and marmalade.

2 Place a griddle over medium-high heat until hot. Lightly oil the griddle. One at a time, dip the sandwiches in the egg mixture and turn gently to coat evenly, keeping the sandwiches intact. Let stand until the bread has soaked up some of the egg mixture, about 30 seconds. Remove the sandwiches from the egg mixture, letting the excess drip back into the bowl, and place on the hot griddle. Cook until the bottoms are golden brown, about 2 minutes. Flip the sandwiches and brown the other sides, about 2 minutes more. Transfer to the baking sheet. When all 4 sandwiches are on the sheet, place the sheet in the oven and bake until the cream cheese melts, about 10 minutes.

3 Serve the French toast sandwiches at once with butter and maple syrup.

variation Experiment with other fruit preserves, such as raspberry or apricot, in place of the orange marmalade.

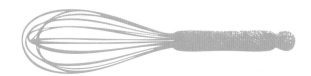

BUTTERMILK FLAPJACKS

2 cups (10 oz/315 g)
all-purpose flour

2 tablespoons sugar

1½ teaspoons
baking powder

1 teaspoon baking soda

½ teaspoon fine sea salt

2⅓ cups (19 fl oz/580 ml)
buttermilk, or as needed

3 large eggs, separated

¼ cup (2 oz/60 g)
unsalted butter, melted,
plus room temperature
butter for serving

Canola oil or
Clarified Butter
(page 212) for cooking

Pure maple syrup
for serving

MAKES 6 SERVINGS

One of my greatest pleasures is sinking a fork into a stack
of syrup-drenched buttermilk pancakes on a lazy weekend
morning. Buttermilk contributes to an exceptionally tender
texture and tangy flavor. Fold in berries or chocolate chips,
if you wish, but the classic is hard to resist.

1 Preheat the oven to 200°F (95°C). In a large bowl, sift together the flour,
sugar, baking powder, baking soda, and salt. In a medium bowl, whisk
together the 2⅓ cups buttermilk, the egg yolks, and the melted butter.
Pour the buttermilk mixture into the flour mixture and stir just until
combined. The batter will be very lumpy.

2 In a small bowl, using a clean whisk or a handheld mixer on high speed,
beat the egg whites until stiff peaks form. Stir about one-third of the whites
into the batter to lighten it, then fold in the remaining whites. The batter
will smooth out, but there will still be some visible lumps.

3 Place a griddle over high heat until hot. (To test, flick a little water onto
the griddle. It should skitter across the surface.) Lightly oil the griddle and
have ready a rimmed baking sheet.

4 For each pancake, pour about ⅓ cup (3 fl oz/80 ml) of the batter onto
the griddle and spread it slightly with the back of the measuring cup. Cook
until bubbles form and break on the surface, about 1½ minutes. Flip the
pancakes and cook until the other sides are golden brown, about 1 minute
more. Transfer to the baking sheet and keep warm in the oven. Repeat until
all of the batter is used, oiling the griddle as needed. If the batter begins
to thicken, thin it with a bit more buttermilk. Serve the pancakes piping hot,
with plenty of butter and syrup.

variation Stir 2 cups (8 oz/250 g) fresh or frozen blueberries or
raspberries, or diced ripe bananas, into the batter. Or add 1 cup (6 oz/185 g)
chocolate chips to the batter.

DAILY CAFE PORTLAND, OR

The motto of the Daily Cafe is "Where we cook what we want to eat," and it is a mouthwatering slogan indeed. With three locations scattered throughout the city, the cafes provide an ever-evolving menu of simply delicious fare. During the week, Portland citizens stop in for gourmet renditions of grab-and-go food like breakfast panini and tempting housemade pastries, or they sit down during lunch to munch on inspired salads or one of the innovative burger specials. On Sundays, the restaurant rolls out a more extensive brunch menu, which spotlights Americana-inspired classics such as eggs, griddlecakes, and in true Northwest style, so-named "fabulous" fruit and nut granola. Founders James Harris and Jamey Sherman pride themselves on sourcing the very best ingredients from local farmers and ranchers, as exemplified by the whole wheat pancakes topped with strawberry and rhubarb compote, a seasonal specialty that showcases some of the Pacific Northwest's glorious spring produce.

WHOLE WHEAT PANCAKES
WITH STRAWBERRY-RHUBARB COMPOTE

1 lb (500 g) rhubarb

¾ cup (6 oz/185 g) plus
2 tablespoons sugar

Finely grated zest
of 1 orange

¼ cup (2 fl oz/60 ml)
fresh orange juice

1 pint (8 oz/250 g)
strawberries,
hulled and sliced

1 cup (5 oz/155 g)
whole wheat flour

1 cup (5 oz/155 g)
all-purpose flour

1 tablespoon
baking powder

1½ teaspoons baking soda

1½ teaspoons kosher salt

1 cup (2½ oz/75 g)
wheat bran

1¾ cups (14 fl oz/430 ml)
whole milk

¾ cup (6 oz/185 g)
plain yogurt

½ cup (4 fl oz/125 ml)
buttermilk, or as needed

3 large eggs

6 tablespoons (3 oz/90 g)
unsalted butter,
melted and cooled,
plus room temperature
butter for serving

Canola oil or
Clarified Butter
(page 212) for cooking

MAKES 4 SERVINGS

1 Trim the rhubarb, cut the stalks into 1-inch (2.5-cm) lengths, and set aside. In a heavy saucepan, combine the ¾ cup sugar with 2 tablespoons water. Cook over high heat, stirring constantly, until the sugar melts. Continue cooking, without stirring, washing down any sugar crystals that form inside the pan with a pastry brush dipped in cold water and occasionally swirling the pan by its handle, until the mixture caramelizes and turns dark amber. Add the sliced rhubarb. The caramel will harden. Stir vigorously until the caramel melts again. Stir in the orange zest and juice. Cook just until the caramel mixture is syrupy and the rhubarb is tender but holds its shape, about 3 minutes. Transfer to a serving bowl and cool slightly. Stir in the strawberries and set aside.

2 Preheat the oven to 200°F (95°C). Have ready a rimmed baking sheet. In a large bowl, sift together the whole wheat flour, all-purpose flour, 2 tablespoons sugar, the baking powder, baking soda, and salt. Add any bran left in the sifter from the wheat flour, and the 1 cup wheat bran. In another bowl, whisk together the milk, yogurt, buttermilk, eggs, and melted butter. Pour the milk mixture into the flour mixture and stir just until combined. Do not overmix.

3 Place a griddle over high heat until hot. (To test, flick a little water onto the griddle. It should skitter across the surface.) Lightly oil the griddle. For each pancake, pour about ¼ cup (2 fl oz/60 ml) of the batter onto the griddle and spread it slightly with the back of the measuring cup. Cook until bubbles form and break on the surface, about 2 minutes. Flip the pancakes and cook until the other sides are golden brown, 1–2 minutes more. Transfer to the baking sheet and keep warm in the oven. Repeat until all of the batter is used, oiling the griddle as needed. If the batter begins to thicken, thin it with a little more buttermilk. Serve the pancakes piping hot, with the warm compote and butter.

POTATO PANCAKES

WITH APPLESAUCE AND SOUR CREAM

Applesauce

2 lb (1 kg) apples, peeled, cored, and cut into cubes

3 tablespoons sugar, or to taste

Finely grated zest of ½ lemon

2 tablespoons fresh lemon juice

2-inch (5-cm) cinnamon stick

Potato Pancakes

2 lb (1 kg) russet potatoes, peeled

1 yellow onion

2 large eggs, beaten

2 tablespoons dried bread crumbs or matzo meal

Kosher salt and freshly ground pepper

Canola oil for frying

Sour cream for serving

2 green onions, white and green parts, thinly sliced (optional)

MAKES 4 SERVINGS

I serve these irresistible, crispy-edged potato pancakes the traditional way, with a dollop of sour cream and applesauce. Nearly any apple will work for the sauce—Jonathan, Gala, Fuji, and Golden Delicious are all good—just taste and adjust the amount of sugar as needed.

1 To make the applesauce, in a medium saucepan, combine the apples, ¼ cup (2 fl oz/60 ml) water, 3 tablespoons sugar, the lemon zest and juice, and the cinnamon stick. Bring to a boil over medium heat, stirring occasionally to dissolve the sugar. Cover and reduce the heat to medium-low. Cook, stirring occasionally, until the apples become tender and break down into a sauce, about 15 minutes. Taste and stir in more sugar, if desired. Remove the cinnamon stick. Set aside.

2 To make the pancakes, preheat the oven to 200°F (95°F). Line a rimmed baking sheet with a wire rack. Line another rimmed baking sheet with paper towels.

3 Using a food processor fitted with the shredding disk, or the large holes of a box grater-shredder, shred the potatoes and then the onion. A handful at a time, squeeze the potato mixture to remove as much moisture as possible, reserving the liquid in a small bowl and transferring the squeezed potato mixture to a larger bowl. Don't be concerned if the potatoes discolor. Let the liquid stand for a couple of minutes. Pour off and discard the reddish liquid, reserving the potato starch in the bottom of the bowl. Scrape the potato starch into the shredded potato mixture. Add the eggs, bread crumbs, 1 teaspoon salt, and ¼ teaspoon pepper and mix well.

4 Pour oil to a depth of about ¼ inch (6 mm) into a large, heavy frying pan and heat over medium-high heat until the oil shimmers. For each pancake, spoon about ¼ cup (1 oz/30 g) of the potato mixture into the oil and spread into a round. Cook until the bottoms are golden brown, about 2½ minutes. Turn the pancakes and cook until the other sides are brown, about 2½ minutes more. Transfer to the rack and keep warm in the oven. Repeat until all of the potato mixture is used, adding more oil as needed.

5 Just before serving, transfer the pancakes to the paper towel–lined baking sheet to briefly drain. Serve immediately, with applesauce and sour cream on the side. Garnish with the green onions, if desired.

GINGERBREAD-SPICED
APPLE PANCAKES

1 cup (8 fl oz/250 ml)
apple juice

1 cup (11 oz/345 g)
pure maple syrup

2 Golden Delicious or
Granny Smith apples,
peeled and cored

2¼ cups (11½ oz/360 g)
all-purpose flour

¼ cup (2 oz/60 g) firmly
packed light brown sugar

2 teaspoons baking powder

¼ teaspoon baking soda

½ teaspoon
ground cinnamon

½ teaspoon
ground allspice

½ teaspoon ground ginger

¼ teaspoon
freshly grated nutmeg

½ teaspoon fine sea salt

1¾ cups (14 fl oz/430 ml)
whole milk, or as needed

2 large eggs

2 tablespoons unsalted
butter, melted, plus
room temperature butter
for serving

Canola oil or
Clarified Butter
(page 212) for cooking

MAKES 4 SERVINGS

When apples are at their peak in the autumn months, I look for all kinds of ways to use them in my cooking—they always make a welcome addition to breakfast. These pancakes, redolent of warm spices, feature a double dose of apples, with shredded fruit in the batter and a splash of juice to augment the flavor of the maple syrup.

◇◇◇

1 In a small saucepan, bring the apple juice to a boil over high heat. Boil until reduced to about ⅓ cup (3 fl oz/80 ml), about 10 minutes. Remove from the heat and whisk in the maple syrup. Cover and set aside to keep warm.

2 Preheat the oven to 200°F (95°C). Have ready a rimmed baking sheet. Using a food processor fitted with the shredding disk, or the large holes of a box grater-shredder,shred the apples. You should have about 1½ cups (6 oz/185 g). In a large bowl, sift together the flour, brown sugar, baking powder, baking soda, cinnamon, allspice, ginger, nutmeg, and salt, rubbing the brown sugar through the mesh with your fingers. In a medium bowl, whisk together the milk, eggs, and melted butter. Pour over the flour mixture and add the shredded apples. Stir just until combined. Do not overmix.

3 Place a griddle over high heat until hot. (To test, flick a little water onto it. It should skitter across the surface.) Lightly oil the griddle. For each pancake, pour about ⅓ cup (3 fl oz/80 ml) of the batter onto the griddle and spread it slightly with the back of the measuring cup. Cook until bubbles form and break on the surface, about 1½ minutes. Flip the pancakes and cook until the other sides are golden brown, about 1 minute more. Transfer to the baking sheet and keep warm in the oven. Repeat until all of the batter is used, oiling the griddle as needed. If the batter begins to thicken, thin it with a bit more milk. Pour the apple-maple syrup into a serving pitcher. Serve the pancakes piping hot, with plenty of butter and the syrup.

SWEDISH PANCAKES
WITH BERRY PRESERVES

1¼ cups (10 fl oz/310 ml) whole milk

3 large eggs

¼ cup (2 fl oz/60 ml) heavy cream

3 tablespoons unsalted butter, melted, plus more melted butter for cooking

1 cup (5 oz/155 g) all-purpose flour

3 tablespoons granulated sugar

¼ teaspoon fine sea salt

About 1 cup (10 oz/315 g) lingonberry, raspberry, or strawberry preserves

Confectioners' sugar for serving

MAKES 4 SERVINGS

To me, Swedish pancakes are decadently old-fashioned. Slightly thicker than crepes, they make ideal bases on which to slather fruit preserves. Scandinavian cooks traditionally spread them with tart-sweet lingonberry preserves, but raspberry or strawberry preserves are just as delicious.

1 In a blender, combine the milk, eggs, cream, and the 3 tablespoons melted butter. Add the flour, granulated sugar, and salt. Blend until smooth, occasionally stopping the blender to scrape down the sides as necessary. Let stand for 10 minutes.

2 Lightly brush a 7–inch (18–cm) nonstick frying pan with melted butter and place over medium–high heat until hot. Pour ¼ cup (2 fl oz/60 ml) of the batter into the pan and tilt the pan to cover the bottom evenly. Drizzle a little batter into any holes. Cook until the bottom is golden brown, about 1 minute. Flip and cook the other side until golden, 1-2 minutes more. Transfer to a plate. Repeat with the remaining batter, adding more butter to the pan as needed and stacking the pancakes, separated by parchment paper, as they are ready. You should have 12 pancakes.

3 Preheat the oven to 350°F (180°C). Have ready a rimmed baking sheet. Place 1 pancake, spotted side up, on a work surface. Spread a generous tablespoon of the preserves onto the center of the pancake. Roll up into a cylinder. Place on the baking sheet. Repeat with the remaining pancakes and preserves. Bake just until hot, about 5 minutes. To serve, place 3 rolled pancakes on each plate and sift confectioners' sugar over the top. Serve at once.

CORNMEAL JOHNNYCAKES

1 tablespoon canola oil

4 thick slices applewood-smoked bacon, coarsely chopped

1²/₃ cups (12 oz/375 g) white cornmeal, preferably stone-ground

⅓ cup (2 oz/60 g) all-purpose flour

1 teaspoon sugar

1 teaspoon baking powder

½ teaspoon fine sea salt

1½ cups (12 fl oz/375 ml) whole milk

2 large eggs

1 cup (4 oz/125 g) shredded sharp Cheddar cheese

Unsalted butter, at room temperature, for serving

Honey, pure cane syrup, or pure maple syrup for serving

MAKES 4 SERVINGS

A uniquely New England tradition, johnnycakes are thought to have first originated in Rhode Island. The subtle crunch of cornmeal gives them appealing texture and a bit of heft. This version, embellished with crisp bits of bacon and sharp Cheddar cheese and served with honey or syrup, makes a delightful sweet-and-salty breakfast treat.

1 Preheat the oven to 200°F (95°C). Have ready a rimmed baking sheet. In a large frying pan, heat the oil over medium heat. Add the bacon and cook, stirring, until crisp and golden, about 6 minutes. Using a slotted spoon, transfer the bacon to paper towels to drain. Pour off and reserve the fat, leaving a film of fat in the pan.

2 In a large bowl, whisk together the cornmeal, flour, sugar, baking powder, and salt. In a medium bowl, whisk together the milk, eggs, and 2 tablespoons of the reserved bacon fat. Pour the milk mixture into the flour mixture and whisk just until combined. Fold in the bacon and cheese.

3 Reheat the frying pan over medium heat until hot. For each johnnycake, pour about ¼ cup (2 fl oz/60 ml) of the batter into the pan and cook until bubbles form on the surface, about 1½ minutes. Flip and cook the other sides until golden, about 1 minute more. Transfer to the baking sheet and keep warm in the oven. Repeat until all the batter is used, greasing the pan with more reserved fat, as needed. Serve the johnnycakes piping hot, with plenty of butter and honey.

variation For a spicier version of these johnnycakes, stir 1 seeded and minced jalapeño chile into the batter.

LEMON-RICOTTA PANCAKES
WITH BERRY COMPOTE

3 cups (12 oz/375 g)
blackberries and/or
raspberries

1/2 cup (5 1/2 oz/170 g)
pure maple syrup

15 oz (470 g) ricotta cheese

1/3 cup (2 oz/60 g)
all-purpose flour

3 large eggs, separated,
at room temperature

3 tablespoons sugar

2 tablespoons
unsalted butter, melted

Finely grated zest
of 1 lemon

1 teaspoon pure
vanilla extract

Canola oil or
Clarified Butter
(page 212) for cooking

MAKES 4 SERVINGS

Ricotta cheese lends a delicate, airy texture to these mini pancakes, and freshly grated lemon zest adds a hint of citrus flavor. Served with a warm compote of fresh tart-sweet berries, they are the perfect fare for a light summer meal. Blueberries can also be used in place of, or along with, the blackberries and/or raspberries.

1 Combine the berries and maple syrup in a saucepan over medium heat. Cook, stirring occasionally, just until the berries begin to release some juices, about 3 minutes. Set aside in the saucepan and keep warm.

2 Preheat the oven to 200°F (95°C). In a medium bowl, whisk together the ricotta, flour, egg yolks, sugar, melted butter, lemon zest, and vanilla. In another bowl, using a clean whisk or a handheld mixer on high speed, beat the egg whites until soft peaks form. Scoop the whites onto the batter, and using the whisk, fold them in evenly.

3 Place a griddle over medium heat until hot. Lightly oil the griddle. Have ready a rimmed baking sheet. For each pancake, pour about 1/4 cup (2 fl oz/60 ml) of the batter onto the griddle and cook until bubbles form on the surface, about 1 1/2 minutes. Flip the pancakes and cook until the other sides are golden, about 1 minute more. Transfer to the baking sheet and keep warm in the oven. Repeat until all of the batter is used, oiling the griddle as needed.

4 Pour the warm berry compote into a serving bowl. Serve the pancakes piping hot, with the compote on the side.

variation The pancakes are equally delicious served with fresh, uncooked fruit, such as sliced peaches, apricots, or plums.

HIGHLAND BAKERY ATLANTA, GA

Located in Atlanta's historic Old Fourth Ward, Highland Bakery inhabits a corner bakery that dates back to the early twentieth century. Owner Stacey Eames first became known for her coffee carts, but when the Old Fourth Ward location became available, she jumped headfirst into the adventure of opening a full-service bakery and restaurant. The cozy, sun-filled dining room quickly became the place to go for a top-notch breakfast, and its success led Eames to open up another location in the Midtown district. The menu is heavily influenced by the Southern food Eames learned to cook from her mother and grandmother, featuring an array of delicious baked goods as well as comforting dishes like peanut butter-stuffed French toast—accompanied, of course, by a mean cappuccino or latte. The gently spiced sweet potato pancakes, one of Highland Bakery's signature breakfast dishes, represent the best of down-home Southern cooking, with a topping of toasted pecans and a drizzle of buttery brown-sugar sauce.

SWEET POTATO PANCAKES
WITH PECANS AND BROWN-SUGAR SAUCE

2 sweet potatoes
(1¼ lb/625 g total),
scrubbed but unpeeled

¾ cup (6 oz/185 g)
unsalted butter,
at room temperature,
plus more for serving

1 cup (7 oz/220 g) plus
2 tablespoons firmly
packed light brown sugar

1½ cups (12 fl oz/375 ml)
whole milk, or as needed

2 large eggs

1½ teaspoons
pure vanilla extract

¾ cup (4 oz/125 g)
whole wheat flour

¾ cup (4 oz/125 g)
all-purpose flour

1 tablespoon
baking powder

½ teaspoon
ground cinnamon

½ teaspoon freshly
grated nutmeg

½ teaspoon fine sea salt

Canola oil or
Clarified Butter
(page 212) for cooking

½ cup (2 oz/60 g)
pecans, toasted (page 217)
and coarsely chopped

MAKES 4–6 SERVINGS

1 Preheat the oven to 400°F (200°C). Pierce the sweet potatoes a few times with a fork, place on a rimmed baking sheet, and bake until tender, about 1 hour. (Or, alternatively, microwave the sweet potatoes on high until tender, about 8 minutes.) Split each sweet potato lengthwise and let cool just until easy to handle, then scoop out and reserve 1¼ cups (6 oz/185 g) of the flesh.

2 Meanwhile, make the brown-sugar sauce. In a medium saucepan, melt ½ cup (4 oz/125 g) of the butter over medium heat. Add the 1 cup brown sugar and whisk until melted. Whisk in ¼ cup (2 fl oz/60 ml) water and bring to a simmer. Reduce the heat to low and simmer until the sauce has reduced slightly, 8–10 minutes. Remove from the heat, cover to keep warm, and set aside.

3 Decrease the oven heat to 200°F (95°C). In a food processor fitted with the metal blade, process the reserved warm sweet potato flesh and the remaining ¼ cup (2 oz/60 g) butter until the butter is fully incorporated. Add ½ cup (4 fl oz/125 ml) of the milk, the eggs, the 2 tablespoons brown sugar, and the vanilla, and process until smooth. Transfer to a bowl and whisk in the remaining 1 cup (8 fl oz/250 ml) milk.

4 In a large bowl, sift together the whole wheat flour, all-purpose flour, baking powder, cinnamon, nutmeg, and salt. Add any bran left in the sifter from the wheat flour. Pour the sweet potato mixture into the flour mixture and stir just until combined. Do not overmix.

5 Place a griddle over medium heat until hot. Lightly oil the griddle. Have ready a rimmed baking sheet. For each pancake, pour about ¼ cup (2 fl oz/60 ml) of the batter onto the griddle and cook until bubbles form and break on the surface, about 2½ minutes. Flip the pancakes and cook until the other sides are golden brown, about 2 minutes more. Transfer to the baking sheet and keep warm in the oven. Repeat until all of the batter is used, oiling the griddle as needed. If the batter begins to thicken, thin it with a bit more milk.

6 Whisk the reserved sauce well and pour into a serving pitcher. Serve the pancakes piping hot, sprinkling each serving with the pecans. Pass the warm brown-sugar sauce and butter on the side.

OLD-FASHIONED
BUTTERMILK WAFFLES

2 cups (10 oz/315 g)
all-purpose flour

2 tablespoons
malted milk powder
or granulated sugar

1 tablespoon
baking powder

1 teaspoon baking soda

¼ teaspoon fine sea salt

2¼ cups (18 fl oz/560 ml)
buttermilk

3 tablespoons unsalted
butter, melted, plus
room temperature butter
for serving

3 large eggs, separated,
at room temperature

1 teaspoon pure
vanilla extract

Canola oil for cooking,
if needed

Pure maple syrup
for serving

MAKES 4 SERVINGS

The secret to creating waffles with a classic, diner-style flavor is to add malted milk powder to the batter, which delivers a touch of sweetness. The toasty aroma rising from the hot waffle iron will tempt even the latest risers out of bed. Serve with plenty of real maple syrup and butter.

1 Preheat the oven to 200°F (95°C) and have ready a rimmed baking sheet. Preheat a regular (not Belgian) waffle iron.

2 In a bowl, sift together the flour, malted milk powder, baking powder, baking soda, and salt. In another bowl, whisk together the buttermilk, melted butter, egg yolks, and vanilla. Add to the flour mixture and stir just until combined. The batter will be quite lumpy. In a small bowl, using a clean whisk or a handheld mixer on high speed, beat the egg whites until soft peaks form. Scoop the whites onto the batter and, using the whisk, gently fold them in evenly. The finished batter may have a few small lumps.

3 If your waffle iron is not nonstick, lightly oil the grid. Ladle some of the batter over the grid, close the lid, and cook until the waffle is golden brown, about 4 minutes. Transfer to the baking sheet and keep warm in the oven. Repeat with the remaining batter. Serve the waffles piping hot with plenty of butter and maple syrup.

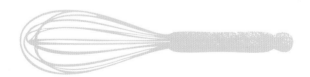

RAISED BELGIAN WAFFLES
WITH STRAWBERRIES AND WHIPPED CREAM

1 lb (500 g) strawberries, hulled and sliced

3 tablespoons granulated sugar

1 package (2¼ teaspoons) active dry yeast

¼ cup (2 fl oz/60 ml) warm (105°– 115°F/ 40°–46°C) water

1¼ cups (10 fl oz/310 ml) whole milk

½ cup (4 fl oz/125 ml) sparkling water

½ cup (4 oz/125 g) unsalted butter, melted and cooled

4 large eggs, separated

1 teaspoon pure vanilla extract

2½ cups (12½ oz/390 g) all-purpose flour

½ teaspoon fine sea salt

Canola oil for cooking, if needed

Confectioners' sugar for serving

Sweetened Whipped Cream (page 216) for serving

MAKES 4 SERVINGS

Belgian waffles are thicker than the classic variety, due to uniquely deep-welled waffle irons. Adding yeast and sparkling water to the batter yields an especially light and airy texture. Fresh strawberries and sweet whipped cream are classic toppings, but these are also delicious drizzled with maple syrup or melted chocolate.

1 In a bowl, toss together the strawberries and 1 tablespoon of the granulated sugar. Let stand at room temperature until the berries give off some juices, at least 1 hour and up to 3 hours.

2 In a small bowl, sprinkle the yeast over the warm water and let stand until foamy, about 5 minutes. Stir until the yeast dissolves. In a large bowl, whisk the milk, sparkling water, butter, egg yolks, the remaining 2 tablespoons granulated sugar, and the vanilla just until combined. Whisk in the dissolved yeast. Add the flour and salt and whisk until smooth. Cover with plastic wrap. Let stand in a warm place until the mixture has risen and the surface has bubbles on it, about 1½ hours.

3 Preheat the oven to 200°F (95°C) and have ready a rimmed baking sheet. Preheat a Belgian waffle iron.

4 Using a clean whisk or handheld mixer on high speed, beat the egg whites in a medium bowl until soft peaks form. Scoop the whites over the batter and, using the whisk, fold them in evenly.

5 If your waffle iron is not nonstick, lightly oil the grid. Ladle some of the batter over the grid, close the lid, and cook until the waffle is golden brown, about 4 minutes. Transfer to the baking sheet and keep warm in the oven. Repeat with the remaining batter. For each serving, sift confectioners' sugar over the waffles, then top with the whipped cream and the strawberries with their juices.

variation Instead of the berries and cream, top the waffles with caramelized bananas and chocolate sauce (see page 42).

SUGAR-AND-SPICE
PUMPKIN WAFFLES

2 cups (10 oz/315 g) all-purpose flour

⅓ cup (3 oz/90 g) sugar

2 teaspoons baking powder

½ teaspoon ground cinnamon

½ teaspoon ground ginger

½ teaspoon fine sea salt

5 tablespoons (2½ oz/75 g) unsalted butter, cut into tablespoons, chilled, plus room temperature butter for serving

1½ cups (12 fl oz/375 ml) whole milk

½ cup (4 oz/125 g) canned pumpkin purée

2 large eggs

Canola oil for cooking, if needed

Pure maple syrup for serving

MAKES 4 SERVINGS

Filled with puréed pumpkin and spices, these pancakes are a celebration of the autumn season. Keep this recipe in mind when you need something special to serve to house guests over a holiday weekend. Make the cranberry syrup (see variation) for a Thanksgiving-inspired breakfast.

1 Preheat the oven to 200°F (95°F) and have ready a rimmed baking sheet. Preheat a waffle iron.

2 In a food processor fitted with the metal blade, pulse the flour, sugar, baking powder, cinnamon, ginger, and salt together until combined. Add the 5 tablespoons butter and pulse about 10 times, until the mixture looks like coarse bread crumbs with some small pea-size pieces of butter. Transfer to a large bowl. (Or, alternatively, in a large bowl, sift together the flour, sugar, baking powder, cinnamon, ginger, and salt. Using a pastry blender or 2 knives, cut the butter into the flour mixture just until the mixture looks like coarse bread crumbs with some small pea-size pieces of butter.)

3 In a medium bowl, whisk together the milk, pumpkin purée, and eggs. Add to the flour mixture and whisk just until combined, but still a little lumpy.

4 If your waffle iron is not nonstick, lightly oil the grid. Ladle some of the batter over the grid, close the lid, and cook until the waffle is golden brown, about 4 minutes. Transfer to the baking sheet and keep warm in the oven. Repeat with the remaining batter. Serve the waffles piping hot with the syrup and butter.

variation To make cranberry syrup, in a saucepan, combine 1 cup (4 oz/125 g) fresh or frozen cranberries, 1 cup (11 oz/345 g) pure maple syrup, and 2 tablespoons sugar and bring to a boil over medium heat. Reduce the heat to medium-low and simmer, stirring occasionally, until the cranberries have popped, about 5 minutes. Transfer to a serving pitcher and serve at once with the waffles.

BANANA–BROWN BUTTER WAFFLES
WITH DULCE DE LECHE

1 cup (8 fl oz/250 ml)
dulce de leche

2½ cups (20 fl oz/625 ml)
whole milk, or as needed

¼ cup (2 oz/60 g)
unsalted butter,
plus room temperature
butter for serving

2 large eggs, separated

1 teaspoon pure
vanilla extract

2 cups (10 oz/315 g)
all-purpose flour

3 tablespoons sugar

4 teaspoons baking powder

¼ teaspoon fine sea salt

2 ripe bananas,
peeled and thinly sliced

Canola oil for cooking,
if needed

MAKES 4 SERVINGS

If I were forced to choose, this might be my favorite waffle recipe. Luscious, thick *dulce de leche*, a caramel made from sweetened milk, is a decadent departure from maple syrup; you can find it in cans or jars in well-stocked groceries and Latin markets. The browned butter adds a nutty flavor to the waffles, and bananas are the final touch.

1 Preheat the oven to 200°F (95°C) and have ready a rimmed baking sheet. Preheat a waffle iron.

2 In a small saucepan, heat the *dulce de leche* over medium heat, stirring frequently, until warm and melted. Gradually whisk in about ½ cup (4 fl oz/125 ml) of the milk, or enough to make a pourable sauce about the thickness of heavy cream. Remove from the heat, cover, and keep warm in the saucepan.

3 In another small saucepan, melt the butter over medium-low heat. Cook, stirring occasionally, until the milk solids in the bottom of the pan turn a toasty brown, about 3 minutes. Transfer to a bowl and let cool slightly. Add the remaining 2 cups (16 fl oz/500 ml) milk, the egg yolks, and the vanilla, and whisk until combined.

4 In a large bowl, sift together the flour, sugar, baking powder, and salt. Add the milk mixture and whisk just until combined (a few lumps are okay). In another bowl, using a clean whisk or a handheld mixer on high speed, beat the egg whites until soft peaks form. Add the sliced bananas to the batter. Scoop the egg whites over the batter and, using the whisk, gently fold the whites and bananas in evenly.

5 If your waffle iron is not nonstick, lightly oil the grid. Ladle some of the batter over the grid, close the lid, and cook until the waffle is golden brown, about 4 minutes. Transfer to the baking sheet and keep warm in the oven. Repeat with the remaining batter. Pour the warm *dulce de leche* sauce into a serving pitcher. Serve the waffles piping hot, with the sauce and butter passed on the side.

GOLDEN CORNMEAL WAFFLES
WITH FRIED CHICKEN

4 boneless, skinless chicken breast halves (about 6 oz/185 g each)

2/3 cup (3 1/2 oz/105 g) plus 3/4 cup (4 oz/125 g) all-purpose flour

2 1/2 teaspoons baking powder

Fine sea salt and freshly ground pepper

2 2/3 cups (21 fl oz/660 ml) buttermilk

Canola oil for deep-frying

1 1/2 cups (10 1/2 oz/330 g) yellow cornmeal, preferably stone-ground

2 tablespoons sugar

1 teaspoon baking soda

6 tablespoons (3 oz/90 g) unsalted butter, melted, plus room temperature butter for serving

2 large eggs, separated

1 cup (6 oz/185 g) fresh or thawed frozen corn kernels

Honey or pure maple syrup for serving

Hot pepper sauce for serving

MAKES 4 SERVINGS

Chicken and waffles is the solution to the ultimate brunch dilemma: sweet or savory? One story claims this retro combination was created to cater to late-night eaters as a compromise between dinner and breakfast. In my experience, everyone can find something to love in the mouthwatering mix of flavors and textures.

1 Using a meat pounder, pound the chicken breast halves until they are a uniform 1/2 inch (12 mm) thick. Have ready a rimmed baking sheet. In a shallow bowl, whisk together the 2/3 cup flour, 1/2 teaspoon of the baking powder, 1/2 teaspoon salt, and 1/2 teaspoon pepper until combined. Pour 2/3 cup (5 fl oz/160 ml) of the buttermilk into a second shallow bowl. One at a time, dip the chicken into the buttermilk, letting the excess liquid drip back into the bowl, then coat the chicken with the seasoned flour, shaking off the excess. Transfer to the baking sheet.

2 Set a wire rack on another rimmed baking sheet and place near the stove. Preheat the oven to 200°F (95°C). Pour oil to a depth of 1/2 inch (12 mm) into a large cast iron or other heavy frying pan and heat over high heat to 375°F (190°C) on a deep-frying thermometer. In batches if necessary, add the chicken pieces and cook, turning once, until golden brown and an instant-read thermometer inserted in the thickest part reads 165°F (74°C), about 8 minutes. Adjust the heat as needed so the oil stays at 375°F. Using tongs, transfer the chicken to the rack to drain. Keep warm in the oven.

3 While the chicken is frying, make the waffles. Have ready a third rimmed baking sheet. Preheat a waffle iron. In a bowl, sift together the 3/4 cup flour, the cornmeal, sugar, remaining 2 teaspoons baking powder, the baking soda, and 1/2 teaspoon salt. In another bowl, whisk together the remaining 2 cups (16 fl oz/500 ml) buttermilk with the melted butter and egg yolks. Add to the cornmeal mixture and stir just until combined (the batter will be lumpy). In a small bowl, using a clean whisk or a handheld mixer on high speed, beat the egg whites until soft peaks form. Scoop the whites over the batter and, using the whisk, gently fold them in evenly. Fold in the corn. The finished batter may retain a few small lumps.

4 If your waffle iron is not nonstick, lightly oil the grid. Ladle some of the batter onto the grid, close the lid, and cook until the waffle is golden brown, about 4 minutes. Transfer to the baking sheet and keep warm in the oven. Repeat with the remaining batter.

5 Serve with butter, honey, and hot pepper sauce.

SARABETH'S NEW YORK, NY

Manhattan may be the last place in America you would expect to find someone making artisan fruit preserves. But that's exactly what Sarabeth Levine was doing in 1981, when she opened up her bakery and jam shop in a small storefront on the Upper West Side. Her family's recipe for orange-apricot marmalade has since expanded into a thriving business that includes several restaurants, a bakery, and a factory that makes her line of spreadable fruit. Sarabeth's restaurants, in particular, have long stood out as welcoming and reliably delicious retreats from the urban bustle of the city. Her cooking style presents the very best renditions of classic recipes—the fluffiest omelets and the lightest pancakes, and croissants and scones that rival any sold in New York (and provide the perfect foundations for generous amounts of her delicious preserves). Patrons have become particularly enamored of her rich, plump cheese-stuffed blintzes, a flawless version of an old New York favorite.

SWEET CHEESE–STUFFED BLINTZES
WITH HONEYED BLUEBERRIES

1½ cups (12 fl oz/375 ml) whole milk

6 large eggs plus 1 large egg yolk

¾ cup (4 oz/125 g) all-purpose flour

1½ teaspoons plus 2 tablespoons granulated sugar

⅛ teaspoon fine sea salt

Clarified Butter (page 212) or canola oil for cooking

¾ lb (375 g) farmer's cheese, at room temperature

½ lb (250 g) cream cheese, at room temperature

Finely grated zest of ½ lemon

1 tablespoon honey

1 pint (8 oz/250 g) blueberries

Sour cream for serving

Confectioners' sugar for serving (optional)

MAKES 4–6 SERVINGS

1 In a large bowl, whisk together the milk and 6 eggs. In another bowl, sift together the flour, 1½ teaspoons granulated sugar, and the salt. Gradually whisk the flour mixture into the egg mixture just until the batter is smooth. With a rubber spatula, rub the batter through a wire sieve into another bowl to remove any lumps.

2 Brush a 7-inch (18-cm) nonstick frying pan with clarified butter and place over medium-high heat until hot. Pour ¼ cup (2 fl oz/60 ml) of the batter into the pan and tilt the pan to coat the bottom evenly, pouring out any excess batter. Drizzle a little batter into any holes. Cook until the bottom |is golden brown, about 1 minute. Flip and cook the other side until golden, about 1 minute more. Transfer to a plate. Repeat with the remaining batter, adding more butter to the pan as needed and stacking the blintzes, separated by parchment paper, as they are ready. You should have 12 blintzes, with a couple of extra to allow for practice. (The blintzes can be prepared, covered tightly with plastic wrap, and refrigerated up to 1 day ahead.)

3 To make the filling, in a bowl, mash together the farmer's cheese and cream cheese with a rubber spatula until combined. Stir in the egg yolk, 2 tablespoons granulated sugar, and the lemon zest. Cover and refrigerate the filling until chilled, at least 1 hour or up to 12 hours.

4 Place 1 blintz, spotted side up, on a work surface. Place about 2 tablespoons of the cheese filling just below the center of the blintz, fold in the sides, and then roll up from the bottom, enclosing the filling. Repeat with the remaining blintzes and filling.

5 Preheat the oven to 200°F (95°C). Have ready a rimmed baking sheet. In a large frying pan, heat 2 tablespoons clarified butter over medium heat. In batches, add the blintzes to the pan and cook, seam side down, until the bottoms are golden, about 2 minutes. Adjust the heat as needed so the blintzes cook steadily to heat the filling without getting too brown. Flip the blintzes over and cook until the other sides are golden, about 2 minutes more. Transfer to the baking sheet and keep warm in the oven. Repeat with the remaining blintzes, adding more clarified butter to the pan as needed.

6 In the same frying pan, warm the honey over medium-low heat. Stir in the blueberries and cook just until heated through, about 1 minute. To serve, place 2 or 3 blintzes on each plate. Top with the blueberries, sour cream, and confectioners' sugar, if using. Serve at once.

BANANA-CHOCOLATE CREPES
WITH TOASTED HAZELNUTS

6 tablespoons (3 oz/90 g) unsalted butter, melted

1¼ cups (10 fl oz/310 ml) whole milk

2 large eggs

1 teaspoon sugar

¼ teaspoon fine sea salt

1 cup (5 oz/155 g) all-purpose flour

Canola oil or Clarified Butter (page 212) for cooking

¾ cup (6 fl oz/180 ml) heavy cream

¼ lb (125 g) bittersweet chocolate, coarsely chopped

2 bananas, peeled and sliced

1 tablespoon firmly packed light brown sugar

¼ cup (2 oz/60 g) toasted, skinned, and chopped hazelnuts (page 217)

MAKES 4 SERVINGS

A breakfast that includes chocolate is an indulgence, so these are a good choice for a special occasion. Wrap and freeze any unused crepes for another meal.

1   In a blender, combine 2 tablespoons of the melted butter, 1 cup (8 fl oz/ 250 ml) plus 2 tablespoons of the milk, the eggs, sugar, and salt. Add the flour and process until smooth, occasionally stopping the blender to scrape down the sides as necessary. Pour into a bowl and cover. Refrigerate for at least 2 hours or up to overnight.

2   Lightly oil an 8-inch (20-cm) crepe or nonstick frying pan and place over medium-high heat until hot. Add the remaining 2 tablespoons milk to the batter and whisk well. Pour ¼ cup (2 fl oz/60 ml) of the batter into the pan and tilt the pan to cover the bottom evenly. Drizzle a little batter into any holes. Cook until the bottom is golden brown, about 1 minute. Flip and cook the other side until golden, about 1 minute more. Transfer to a plate. Repeat with the remaining batter, adding more oil to the pan as needed and stacking the crepes, separated by parchment or waxed paper, as they are ready. You should have 8 crepes. Set the crepes aside. (The crepes can be made up to 2 days ahead, covered with plastic wrap, and refrigerated.)

3   In a small saucepan, bring the cream to a simmer over medium heat. Remove from the heat and add the chocolate. Let stand for 3 minutes, then whisk until smooth. Cover and set aside to keep warm.

4   In a frying pan, add 2 tablespoons of the melted butter and warm over medium heat. Add the bananas and cook, stirring gently, until heated through, about 2 minutes. Add the brown sugar and cook until it melts, about 1 minute. Remove from the heat.

5   Preheat the oven to 350°F (180°C). Lightly brush a rimmed baking sheet with some of the remaining 2 tablespoons melted butter. Place 1 crepe on a work surface. Place a few caramelized banana slices on the lower right quadrant of the crepe. Fold the crepe in half from left to right, then in half again from top to bottom to cover the bananas and form a triangle. Place on the prepared baking sheet. Repeat with the remaining crepes and bananas. Brush the tops of the filled crepes with the remaining melted butter. Bake just until hot throughout, about 5 minutes.

6   To serve, place 2 crepes on each plate. Drizzle with the chocolate sauce, then sprinkle with hazelnuts. Serve at once.

BUCKWHEAT CREPES

WITH HAM, GRUYÈRE, AND FRIED EGGS

6 tablespoons (3 oz/90 g) unsalted butter, melted

1¼ cups (10 fl oz/310 ml) whole milk

9 large eggs

½ teaspoon fine sea salt

½ cup (2½ oz/75 g) buckwheat flour

½ cup (2½ oz/75 g) all-purpose flour

Canola oil or Clarified Butter (page 212) for cooking

1½ cups (6 oz/185 g) shredded Gruyère cheese

12 thin slices Black Forest ham

Kosher salt and freshly ground pepper

MAKES 6 SERVINGS

As a culinary student in Paris, I was so full after cooking all day that dinner was often just this savory crepe, purchased from a street vendor. Here's my simplified version of France's *crêpe complèt*—a buckwheat crepe filled with ham and Gruyère cheese, and topped with a fried egg.

1 In a blender, combine 2 tablespoons of the melted butter, 1 cup (8 fl oz/250 ml) plus 2 tablespoons of the milk, 3 of the eggs, and the salt. Add the buckwheat flour and all-purpose flour and process until smooth, occasionally stopping the blender to scrape down the sides as necessary. Pour into a bowl and cover. Refrigerate for at least 2 hours or up to overnight.

2 Lightly oil an 8-inch (20-cm) crepe or nonstick frying pan and place over medium-high heat until hot. Add the remaining 2 tablespoons milk to the batter and whisk well. Pour ¼ cup (2 fl oz/60 ml) of the batter into the pan and tilt the pan to cover the bottom evenly. Drizzle a little batter into any holes. Cook until the bottom is golden brown, about 1 minute. Flip and cook the other side until golden, about 1 minute more. Transfer to a plate. Repeat with the remaining batter, adding more oil to the pan as needed and stacking the crepes, separated by parchment or waxed paper, as they are ready. You should have 12 crepes. (The crepes can be made up to 2 days ahead, covered with plastic wrap, and refrigerated.)

3 Preheat the oven to 350°F (180°C). Lightly brush a rimmed baking sheet with 1 tablespoon of the melted butter. Place 1 crepe on a work surface. Sprinkle with about 2 tablespoons of the cheese, then top with a slice of ham. Fold the crepe in half, then in half again to form a triangle. Place on the prepared baking sheet. Repeat with the remaining crepes, cheese, and ham. Brush the tops of the filled crepes with 1 tablespoon of the melted butter. Bake just until hot throughout, about 5 minutes.

4 In a large frying pan, warm the remaining 2 tablespoons melted butter over medium heat until the butter is foamy. One at a time, crack the remaining 6 eggs into the pan. Season with salt and pepper, cover, reduce the heat to medium-low, and cook until the whites are set, about 2 minutes for sunny-side-up eggs. Or carefully flip the eggs and cook to the desired doneness.

5 To serve, place 2 crepes on each plate and top with a fried egg. Serve at once.

variation Substitute smoked turkey and Cheddar for the ham and Gruyère.

2

EGGS, GLORIOUS EGGS

TOMATO AND BASIL SCRAMBLE

WITH FRESH MOZZARELLA

2 teaspoons olive oil

1 tablespoon
minced shallot

1 cup (6 oz/185 g) cherry
or grape tomatoes, halved

Kosher salt and
freshly ground pepper

12 large eggs

2 tablespoons
chopped fresh basil

1 tablespoon
unsalted butter

¼ lb (125 g) fresh
mozzarella, cubed

MAKES 4 SERVINGS

This colorful scramble is easy to toss together; the trick is to scramble the eggs until barely set, remove the pan from the stove top, and let the eggs finish cooking with the residual heat of the pan. This is my go-to egg dish during the summer, when the cherry tomatoes and sweet-scented basil in the pots on my deck boast their fullest flavors.

1 In a frying pan, preferably nonstick, heat the oil over medium heat. Add the shallot and cook, stirring occasionally, until softened, about 1 minute. Add the cherry tomatoes and cook until hot and beginning to soften, about 2 minutes. Remove from the heat and season with salt and pepper. Transfer the tomato mixture to a bowl and cover to keep warm.

2 In a bowl, whisk together the eggs, 1 tablespoon of the basil, ¾ teaspoon salt, and ¼ teaspoon pepper just until thoroughly blended. Do not overbeat.

3 Add the butter to the frying pan and melt over medium–low heat. When the butter is hot, add the egg mixture to the pan and cook until the eggs begin to set, about 20 seconds. Stir with a heatproof spatula, scraping up the eggs on the bottom and sides of the pan and folding them toward the center. Repeat until the eggs are barely cooked into moist curds. Add the cherry tomato mixture and the mozzarella and stir to distribute throughout the eggs. Remove the pan from the heat and let the eggs stand in the pan to allow the residual heat to finish cooking them and melt the mozzarella, about 1 minute.

4 Sprinkle the remaining 1 tablespoon basil over the scramble and serve at once.

POTATO, EGG, AND CHEESE
BREAKFAST TACOS

2 large russet potatoes,
scrubbed but unpeeled

2 tablespoons olive oil

1 small yellow onion,
chopped

Kosher salt and
freshly ground pepper

8 large eggs

1 tablespoon
unsalted butter

8 corn or flour tortillas,
each about 6 inches (15 cm)
in diameter, warmed

1 cup (4 oz/125 g)
shredded Monterey jack or
Cheddar cheese

Pico de Gallo (page 213)
for serving

MAKES 4 SERVINGS

Whenever I visit Austin, Texas, I go on a breakfast "taco crawl." There are so many variations on the theme of eggs and tortillas that I can't pick a favorite, but when I want something especially hearty, I like the panfried potatoes mixed into this version. The fresh salsa is essential.

1 Put the potatoes in a large saucepan and add enough cold salted water to cover. Bring to a boil over high heat. Reduce the heat to medium-low and simmer until tender when pierced with the tip of a knife, about 25 minutes. Drain and rinse under cold running water. Refrigerate until chilled, at least 2 hours or up to overnight.

2 Peel the potatoes and cut into small cubes. In a large frying pan, preferably nonstick, heat the oil over medium-high heat. Add the potato cubes and cook, stirring occasionally, until browned, about 10 minutes. Add the onion and cook, stirring often, until softened, about 2 minutes. Remove from the heat and season with salt and pepper.

3 Meanwhile, in a bowl, whisk together the eggs, ¾ teaspoon salt, and ¼ teaspoon pepper just until thoroughly blended. Do not overbeat. Return the pan with the potatoes to medium-low heat. Add the egg mixture to the pan and cook until the eggs begin to set, about 20 seconds. Stir with a heatproof spatula, scraping up the eggs on the bottom and sides of the pan and folding them toward the center. Repeat until the eggs are barely cooked into moist curds. Remove the pan from the heat and let stand to allow the residual heat to finish cooking the eggs, about 1 minute.

4 Fill the tortillas with equal amounts of the potato-egg mixture, sprinkle with cheese, and top with a spoonful of the pico de gallo. Serve at once.

variation For a heftier taco, add crisp bacon, diced ham, or cooked and crumbled chorizo or sausage to the potato-egg mixture.

TEXAS-STYLE MIGAS
WITH RANCHERO SAUCE

Ranchero Sauce

1 tablespoon canola oil

1 small yellow onion, chopped

½ jalapeño chile, seeded and minced

2 cloves garlic, minced

1 can (14½ oz/455 g) diced tomatoes, undrained

½ cup (4 fl oz/125 ml) canned tomato sauce

1 teaspoon chili powder

1 canned chipotle pepper in adobo, chopped, plus ½ teaspoon adobo sauce (optional)

Kosher salt and freshly ground pepper

Migas

10 large eggs

Kosher salt and freshly ground pepper

2 tablespoons canola oil

2 cups (16 fl oz/500 ml) Pico de Gallo (page 213)

1½ cups (4½ oz/140 g) coarsely broken tortilla chips

½ cup (2 oz/60 g) *each* shredded sharp Cheddar cheese and shredded Monterey jack cheese

MAKES 4 SERVINGS

1 To make the ranchero sauce, in a saucepan, heat the oil over medium heat. Add the onion, chile, and garlic and cook, stirring occasionally, until softened, about 5 minutes. Transfer to a blender. Add the tomatoes and their juices, the tomato sauce, chili powder, and chipotle pepper and sauce, if using, and purée. Return to the saucepan and bring to a boil over high heat. Reduce the heat to medium-low, and cook, stirring frequently, until reduced to about 2 cups (16 fl oz/500 ml), about 30 minutes. Season with salt and pepper. Cover and keep the sauce warm over very low heat.

2 To make the migas, in a large bowl, whisk together the eggs, ½ teaspoon salt, and ¼ teaspoon pepper. In a frying pan, preferably nonstick, heat the oil over medium-high heat. Add half of the pico de gallo and cook until the onion softens, about 1 minute. Add the egg mixture to the pan and cook until the eggs begin to set, about 20 seconds. Stir with a heatproof spatula, scraping up the eggs on the bottom and sides of the pan and folding them toward the center. Repeat until the eggs are just beginning to form moist curds, about 1 minute. Add the tortilla chips and stir to distribute throughout the eggs. Cook, stirring occasionally, until the eggs are barely cooked into moist curds, about 1 minute more. Remove the pan from the heat and let the eggs stand in the pan to allow the residual heat to finish cooking them, about 1 minute.

3 In a bowl, combine the cheeses. Divide the migas among 4 plates. Top each serving with a few tablespoons of the ranchero sauce and ¼ cup (1 oz/30 g) of the cheese. Serve at once with the remaining ranchero sauce and pico de gallo passed on the side.

KERBEY LANE CAFE AUSTIN, TX

In other parts of the country, eggs may be routinely served with toast, but in
Texas, eggs and tortillas go hand in hand. The duo appears on breakfast menus
in countless rib-sticking dishes such as burritos, quesadillas, and tacos. Another
favorite—especially in Austin—is migas, which means "crumbs" in Spanish, but
in the Tex-Mex parlance of the American Southwest the name refers to a tasty
scramble of eggs, strips of crisp corn tortillas, and a mayhem of fresh chiles,
tomatoes, and spices. And no one does migas like Kerbey Lane Cafe. Opening
their doors in 1980, Kerbey Lane has earned status as a local brunch institution,
with an innovative mission that places fresh, local, and affordable food into
the context of a 24-hour diner. Five locations throughout the city each offer
a distinct character, but with a consistently warm and friendly atmosphere.
Breakfast favorites, from fluffy pancakes to all sorts of tortilla-egg combos, are
served round-the-clock to satisfy hungry customers no matter what the hour.

SMOKED SALMON SCRAMBLE
WITH CREAM CHEESE AND HERBS

12 large eggs

2 tablespoons heavy cream

Freshly ground pepper

2 tablespoons
unsalted butter

¼ lb (125 g) sliced
smoked salmon,
roughly chopped

3 oz (90 g) cream cheese,
cubed with a wet knife

1½ teaspoons
chopped fresh chives

1½ teaspoons
minced fresh dill

MAKES 4–6 SERVINGS

For many residents of the New York metropolitan area, including myself, smoked salmon and cream cheese are the perfect mates. The venerable pair appears on many breakfast menus, usually on a bagel, but you can also find them tucked into a fluffy egg scramble such as this one. A sprinkling of chopped fresh chives and dill adds a fresh herbal accent.

1 In a bowl, whisk together the eggs, cream, and ¼ teaspoon pepper just until thoroughly blended. Do not overbeat.

2 In a frying pan, preferably nonstick, melt the butter over medium-low heat until hot. Tilt the pan to cover the bottom evenly with butter. Add the egg mixture to the pan and cook until the eggs begin to set, about 20 seconds. Stir with a heatproof spatula, scraping up the eggs on the bottom and sides of the pan and folding them toward the center. Repeat until the eggs are barely cooked into moist curds. Add the smoked salmon and cream cheese and stir to distribute throughout the eggs. Remove the pan from the heat and let the eggs stand in the pan to allow the residual heat to finish cooking them and warm the salmon and cream cheese, about 1 minute.

3 Combine the chives and dill. Sprinkle over the scramble and serve at once.

variation This scramble is equally delicious made with smoked trout, flaked into chunks, instead of the smoked salmon.

CAJUN SCRAMBLE

WITH SAUSAGE, PEPPERS, AND CHEESE

2 teaspoons olive oil

½ lb (250 g) andouille or other hot smoked sausage, cubed

½ cup (2½ oz/75 g) chopped green bell pepper

½ cup (2½ oz/75 g) chopped red bell pepper

2 green onions, white and green parts, minced

1 clove garlic, minced

12 large eggs

Kosher salt

¼ teaspoon hot pepper sauce

2 tablespoons unsalted butter

½ cup (2 oz/60 g) shredded sharp Cheddar cheese

MAKES 4–6 SERVINGS

Andouille sausage is one of the trademark ingredients of French-inflected Cajun cooking. I love the way it lends a smoky, spicy kick to the dishes in which it is featured. For an authentic spread reminiscent of New Orleans, offer this dish with a batch of beignets (page 130) and a café au lait made with chicory-laced coffee.

1 In a frying pan, preferably nonstick, heat the oil over medium-high heat. Add the andouille and cook, stirring occasionally, until it begins to brown, about 5 minutes. Add the bell peppers and reduce the heat to medium. Cover and cook, stirring occasionally, until the peppers are tender, about 4 minutes. Uncover and add the green onions and garlic. Cook, stirring occasionally, until the garlic softens and is fragrant, about 2 minutes. Transfer the sausage mixture to a bowl and cover with aluminum foil to keep warm.

2 In a bowl, whisk together the eggs, ½ teaspoon salt, and the hot pepper sauce just until thoroughly blended. Do not overbeat.

3 Add the butter to the frying pan and melt over medium-low heat. When the butter is hot, add the egg mixture to the pan and cook until the eggs begin to set, about 20 seconds. Stir with a heatproof spatula, scraping up the eggs on the bottom and sides of the pan and folding them toward the center. Repeat until the eggs are barely cooked into moist curds. Add the sausage mixture and cheese and stir to distribute throughout the eggs. Remove the pan from the heat and let the eggs stand in the pan to allow the residual heat to finish cooking them and melt the cheese, about 1 minute. Serve at once.

variation You can substitute cubed fresh mozzarella cheese for the Cheddar.

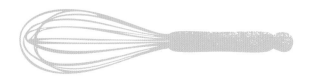

CHILAQUILES

WITH TOMATILLO SALSA AND EGGS

14 corn tortillas,
each cut into sixths

2 cups (16 fl oz/500 ml)
canola oil

2 lb (1 kg) tomatillos,
papery husks removed

1½ cups (6 oz/185 g)
chopped white onions

½ cup (4 fl oz/125 ml)
Chicken Stock (page 214) or
low-sodium chicken broth

⅓ cup (½ oz/15 g)
packed fresh cilantro
leaves, plus chopped
cilantro for garnish

4 cloves garlic,
coarsely chopped

1 jalapeño chile,
seeded and minced

Kosher salt and
freshly ground pepper

3 tablespoons olive oil

6 large eggs

Minced red onion
for garnish

Grated *cotija* or aged
goat cheese for garnish

Crema or sour cream
for garnish

MAKES 4–6 SERVINGS

Here, crisp corn tortilla wedges are simmered in a mild tomatillo salsa, creating a savory base for scrambled eggs. I learned to make the dish when I was studying in Mexico.

1 Preheat the oven to 300°F (150°C). Position one rack in the middle of the oven and a second rack in the top third of the oven. Spread the tortilla wedges on 2 rimmed baking sheets. Bake until the tortillas begin to dry out, about 15 minutes. Remove from the oven and let cool completely.

2 In a heavy frying pan, heat the canola oil over medium-high heat until it shimmers. Working in batches, add the tortilla wedges and fry until golden on one side, about 30 seconds. Turn and fry until golden on the second side, 15–20 seconds. Transfer to paper towels to drain. Repeat with the remaining wedges. Discard the oil in the pan.

3 Bring a large saucepan of water to a boil over high heat. Reduce the heat to medium-high, add the tomatillos, and cook until they soften and become paler in color (but before they burst), about 5 minutes. Using a slotted spoon, transfer the tomatillos to a blender or food processor. Add the white onions, chicken stock, cilantro leaves, garlic, and chile and process until puréed. Season with salt and pepper.

4 Add 2 tablespoons of the olive oil to the pan and heat over medium heat. Add the tomatillo sauce (it will splatter) and bring to a boil. Cook, stirring often, until the sauce has thickened and is reduced by about one-third, about 10 minutes. Reduce the heat to medium-low. A handful at a time, add the tortillas, pressing them with a wooden spoon to submerge them under the simmering sauce. Cook until the tortillas are softened, about 3 minutes. Remove from the heat and cover to keep warm.

5 In a bowl, whisk together the eggs, ¾ teaspoon salt, and ¼ teaspoon pepper just until thoroughly blended. Do not overbeat. In a frying pan, preferably nonstick, warm the remaining 1 tablespoon olive oil over medium-low heat. Add the egg mixture to the pan and cook until the eggs begin to set, about 20 seconds. Stir with a heatproof spatula, scraping up the eggs on the bottom and sides of the pan and folding them toward the center. Repeat until the eggs are barely cooked into moist curds. Remove the pan from the heat and let the eggs stand in the pan to allow the residual heat to finish cooking them, about 1 minute.

6 Spoon the chilaquiles and eggs onto plates. Sprinkle with the red onion, cheese, and cilantro, and drizzle with *crema*. Serve at once.

BLACK BEAN AND CHORIZO
BREAKFAST BURRITOS

¾ lb (375 g) fresh
Mexican-style chorizo
sausage, casings removed

½ cup (2 oz/60 g) chopped
yellow onion

½ cup (2½ oz/75 g)
chopped red bell pepper

1 clove garlic, minced

1 can (15½ oz/485 g)
black beans,
drained and rinsed

Kosher salt and
freshly ground pepper

8 large eggs

2 tablespoons
unsalted butter

4 flour tortillas, each
about 9 inches (23 cm)
in diameter, warmed

1 ripe avocado, pitted,
peeled, and cut
into 8 wedges

½ cup (4 oz/125 g)
sour cream, as needed

½ cup (4 fl oz/125 ml)
Ranchero Sauce (page 52)

MAKES 4 SERVINGS

The ever-popular breakfast burrito varies from cook to cook:
I like mine stuffed with as many fillings as possible—including
scrambled eggs, black beans, avocado, sour cream, and
salsa, and always some spicy chorizo sausage. Dig into
this hefty breakfast wrap, and you probably won't need
to eat again until dinnertime.

1 In a medium frying pan, cook the chorizo over medium-high heat,
breaking it up with the side of a wooden spoon, until it begins to brown,
about 8 minutes. Using a slotted spoon, transfer the chorizo to paper
towels to drain. Pour off all but 1 tablespoon of the fat from the pan.

2 Add the onion and bell pepper and cook, stirring occasionally, until
tender, about 5 minutes. Stir in the garlic and cook until fragrant, about
1 minute. Return the chorizo to the pan. Add the black beans and stir well.
Stir in ½ cup (4 fl oz/125 ml) water. Simmer until the beans are heated
through and the liquid is almost completely evaporated, about 5 minutes.
Season with salt. Remove from the heat and keep warm.

3 In a large bowl, whisk together the eggs, ½ teaspoon salt, and ¼ teaspoon
pepper. In a large frying pan, preferably nonstick, melt the butter over
medium heat. Pour in the eggs and cook until the eggs begin to set, about
20 seconds. Stir with a heatproof spatula, scraping up the eggs on the
bottom and sides of the pan and folding them toward the center. Repeat
until the eggs are barely cooked into moist curds. Remove the pan from
the heat and let the eggs stand in the pan to allow the residual heat to finish
cooking them.

4 Place a warm tortilla on a work surface. Spoon one-fourth of the eggs
on the bottom half, leaving a 1-inch (2.5-cm) border. Top with one-fourth
of the beans, 2 avocado wedges, about 2 tablespoons of the sour cream,
and 2 tablespoons of the sauce. Fold in both sides of the tortilla about 1 inch.
Starting at the bottom, roll up the tortilla to enclose the filling. Repeat with
the remaining ingredients. Serve at once, with the remaining sauce passed
on the side.

variation For a fresh version, substitute Pico de Gallo (page 213) for the
Ranchero Sauce. You may also substitute guacamole for the sliced avocado.

THREE-PEPPER SCRAMBLED EGGS
WITH SMOKED PORK CHOPS

Canola oil for cooking

4 smoked pork chops, cut about ½-inch (12-mm) thick

1 tablespoon unsalted butter

½ cup (2½ oz/75 g) chopped red bell pepper

½ cup (2½ oz/75 g) chopped green bell pepper

1 small onion, chopped

1 jalapeño chile, seeded and minced

8 large eggs

Kosher salt and freshly ground black pepper

MAKES 4 SERVINGS

Brined and smoked like ham, smoked pork chops are an old-fashioned treat with a deeply satisfying flavor—I can never resist gnawing on the tender meat nestled closest to the bone. With a peppery scramble on the side, simple ham and eggs transcend to new heights. Add a side of veggie hash (page 164) if you are really hungry.

1 Lightly oil a large ridged grill pan and heat over medium heat. Add the pork chops and cook, turning once, until seared with grill marks on both sides and heated through, about 10 minutes.

2 Meanwhile, in a frying pan, preferably nonstick, melt the butter over medium heat until hot. Add the bell peppers, onion, and chile. Cook, stirring occasionally, until tender, about 5 minutes.

3 In a bowl, whisk together the eggs, ¾ teaspoon salt, and ¼ teaspoon pepper. Do not overbeat. Add the eggs to the frying pan and cook until they begin to set, about 20 seconds. Stir with a heatproof spatula, scraping up the eggs on the bottom and sides of the pan and folding them toward the center. Repeat until the eggs are barely cooked into moist curds, about 3 minutes. Remove the pan from the heat and let the eggs stand in the pan to allow the residual heat to finish cooking them.

4 Divide the eggs evenly among 4 plates. Add a chop to each plate. Serve at once.

variation If your market doesn't have smoked pork chops, serve the eggs with thick slices of ham that you've seared in a frying pan until browned and heated through.

BREAKFAST QUESADILLAS

WITH CHICKEN, SPINACH, AND AVOCADO

1 skinless, boneless chicken breast half, about 5 oz (155 g)

Kosher salt and freshly ground pepper

4 large eggs

1 tablespoon olive oil

1 cup (2 oz/60 g) coarsely chopped baby spinach

½ cup (3 oz/90 g) seeded and chopped tomatoes

2 large flour tortillas, each about 10 inches (25 cm) in diameter

⅔ cup (2½ oz/75 g) shredded sharp Cheddar cheese

¼ cup (2 oz/60 g) sour cream

1 avocado, pitted, peeled, and sliced

¼ cup (2 fl oz/60 ml) Pico de Gallo (page 213)

MAKES 2–4 SERVINGS

1 Preheat the broiler. Lightly pound the chicken breast half with a flat meat pounder until ½ inch (12 mm) thick. Season with ¼ teaspoon salt and ⅛ teaspoon pepper. Lightly oil a broiler pan. Broil the chicken breast, turning at the halfway point, until lightly browned and firm when pressed in the center, about 10 minutes. Transfer to a chopping board and let cool for 5 minutes. Cut into ½-inch (12-mm) dice. Place in a bowl and set aside.

2 Preheat the oven to 200°F (95°C). In a bowl, whisk together the eggs, ¼ teaspoon salt, and ⅛ teaspoon pepper. In a frying pan, preferably nonstick, heat the oil over medium heat. Add the egg mixture to the pan and cook until the edges begin to set, about 20 seconds. Stir with a heatproof spatula, scraping up the eggs on the bottom and sides of the pan and folding them toward the center. Add the chicken, spinach, and tomatoes, and continue cooking, stirring frequently, until the eggs are barely cooked into moist curds, about 1 minute. Remove the pan from the heat and set aside.

3 Heat another frying pan over medium heat. Have ready a rimmed baking sheet. Place 1 tortilla in the pan and heat until warmed, about 1 minute. Flip the tortilla and sprinkle the bottom half with ⅓ cup (1¼ oz/40 g) of the cheese. Top the cheese with half of the egg mixture. Fold the tortilla in half in the frying pan to cover the cheese and egg mixture. Continue cooking until the underside begins to brown, about 1 minute. Flip and cook the other side until it begins to brown, about 1 minute more. Transfer to the baking sheet and keep warm in the oven. Repeat to make the second quesadilla.

4 Cut each quesadilla into wedges and divide between individual plates. Top each serving with a dollop of sour cream, some avocado slices, and a spoonful of pico de gallo. Serve at once.

BLU JAM CAFE LOS ANGELES, CA

Blu Jam gets its unusual name from the location's former life as an underground blues and jazz club. Still every bit as hip as its namesake, Blu Jam today is tucked among the trendy boutiques of Melrose Avenue, and has a quintessentially laidback L.A. attitude. The pedestrian who tires of shopping and celebrity spotting is easily tempted to relax in the outdoor patio, order up a latte with whimsically designed foam, and enjoy some creative California brunch fare. Slimmed-down dishes include a Tex-Mex tofu burrito and a "muscle beach" egg whites scramble, but the decadent eater has ample options, too. Caramel French toast made of brioche gets rave reviews, and many find guilty pleasure in chef and owner Kamil Majer's infamous macaroni and cheese scramble. But perhaps the best representative of Blu Jam comes as one of the many Latin specialties, such as a cheesy, eggy quesadilla packed with chicken and fresh veggies. Serve with a side of spicy black beans (page 184) for an extra hearty breakfast.

CHEESY EGG SANDWICHES
WITH HOMEMADE SAUSAGE

6 Pork and Sage Sausage
Patties (page 177)

6 slices sharp
Cheddar cheese

6 English muffins,
split in half crosswise

6 large eggs

Kosher salt and freshly
ground pepper

2 tablespoons
unsalted butter

MAKES 6 SERVINGS

You may be able to purchase a pale imitation of this sandwich at a fast-food joint, but it would bear little resemblance to one freshly made in your own kitchen. This recipe is proof that it couldn't be simpler to fry and assemble the ingredients. Within minutes, you'll reap the rewards of egg, sausage, and cheese melding into a savory breakfast eaten out of hand.

1 Prepare and shape the sausage patties as directed. Heat a large frying pan, preferably nonstick, over medium heat. Add the patties and reduce the heat to medium-low. Cook until the undersides are browned, about 5 minutes. Flip the patties and cook until browned on the other sides and the centers feel firm when pressed with your finger, about 5 minutes more. Place a slice of cheese on each patty, cover the pan, and cook until the cheese melts, about 1 minute. Remove the patties from the pan and set aside on a paper towel–lined plate until ready to use. Discard the fat from the pan.

2 Preheat the broiler. Place the muffin halves, cut side up, on a baking sheet and toast in the broiler until lightly crisped, about 2 minutes. Remove and set aside.

3 In a bowl, whisk together the eggs, ¼ teaspoon salt, and a few grinds of pepper just until thoroughly blended. Do not overbeat. Wipe out the frying pan with paper towels. Add the butter and heat over medium heat until melted and hot. Tilt the pan to coat the bottom with the butter. Add the egg mixture to the pan and cook until the eggs have barely begun to set around the edges, about 30 seconds. Using a heatproof spatula, lift the cooked edges and gently push them towards the center, tilting the pan to allow the liquid egg on top to flow underneath, then cook for about 30 seconds. Repeat the process again, but this time cover the frying pan, and cook until the eggs have set into a thin omelet, about 30 seconds longer. Remove from the heat. Using the heatproof spatula, divide the omelet into 6 wedges.

4 Top 6 of the muffin halves with the sausage patties, then a wedge of the eggs, folded to fit. Cover with the remaining muffin halves. Serve at once.

variation Of course, fried eggs (page 211) would be just as delicious as scrambled eggs. And cooked smoked ham or bacon could easily stand in for the sausage.

STEAK AND EGGS
WITH HERBED CHERRY TOMATOES

4 tablespoons
(2 fl oz/60 ml) olive oil

4 small boneless beef
rib-eye or top loin steaks,
about ½ inch (12 mm) thick

Kosher salt and
freshly ground pepper

1½ cups (9 oz/280 g)
cherry tomatoes, halved

1 teaspoon chopped
fresh chives

½ teaspoon minced
fresh thyme

8 large eggs

MAKES 4 SERVINGS

From sausages to bacon, pork may be the king of the breakfast table, but I find that a juicy rib-eye steak with a side of eggs is an awfully tempting combination. Here, a vibrant sauté of cherry tomatoes brightens the classic duo. Serve with toasted English muffins to soak up the juices.

1 In a large heavy frying pan, preferably cast iron, heat 1 tablespoon of the oil over medium-high heat until very hot. Trim the steaks of any surface fat and season with ½ teaspoon salt and ¼ teaspoon pepper. Add the steaks and cook until the undersides are nicely browned, about 3 minutes. Turn and cook until the other sides are browned, about 3 minutes for medium-rare. Transfer the steaks to a plate and tent with aluminum foil to keep warm.

2 In the same pan, heat 2 tablespoons of the oil over medium-high heat. Add the cherry tomatoes, ¼ teaspoon salt, and ⅛ teaspoon pepper. Cook the tomatoes, stirring frequently, just until they begin to soften and give off their juices, about 3 minutes. Stir in the chives and thyme.

3 In another large frying pan, heat the remaining 1 tablespoon oil over medium heat. Crack 4 of the eggs into the pan. Season with salt and pepper, cover, reduce the heat to medium-low, and cook until the whites are set, about 2 minutes for sunny-side-up eggs. Or carefully flip the eggs and cook to the desired doneness. Repeat with the remaining eggs.

4 Place a steak and 2 fried eggs on each of 4 plates and top with the cherry tomatoes. Serve at once.

ASPARAGUS AND FRIED EGGS
WITH PANCETTA AND BREAD CRUMBS

1 lb (500 g) plump
asparagus, trimmed

4 tablespoons
(2 fl oz/60 ml) olive oil

Kosher salt and freshly
ground pepper

¼ lb (125 g) pancetta,
chopped

1 cup (2 oz/60 g) fresh
bread crumbs (page 217)

4 large eggs

Chopped fresh flat-leaf
parsley for serving

MAKES 4 SERVINGS

A simple fried egg is a delight to eat, especially when the buttery yolk mingles with a bed of earthy roasted asparagus spears. Topped with salty pancetta, bread crumbs, and fresh herbs, this is a simple dish with big flavor. I like to make it in the spring when asparagus is at its peak.

1 Preheat the oven to 400°F (200°C). Spread the asparagus in a single layer on a rimmed baking sheet. Drizzle with 1 tablespoon of the oil. Roll the asparagus in the oil until lightly coated. Roast until the asparagus are just tender, about 10 minutes. Season with salt and pepper.

2 Meanwhile, combine the pancetta and 1 tablespoon of the oil in a large frying pan. Cook over medium-high heat, stirring occasionally, until the pancetta is browned, about 8 minutes. Using a slotted spoon, transfer the pancetta to paper towels to drain. Add the bread crumbs to the fat in the pan. Cook, stirring often, until crisp and browned, about 1 minute. Return the pancetta to the pan and stir well. Transfer the pancetta and bread crumbs to a plate.

3 Add the remaining 2 tablespoons oil to the pan and warm over medium heat. One at a time, crack the eggs into the pan. Season with salt and pepper, cover, reduce the heat to medium-low, and cook until the whites are set, about 2 minutes for sunny-side-up eggs. Or carefully flip the eggs and cook to the desired doneness.

4 Divide the asparagus among 4 individual serving dishes or plates. Top each serving with an egg and sprinkle generously with the pancetta and bread crumbs. Garnish with the parsley and serve at once.

HUEVOS RANCHEROS

2 cups (16 fl oz/500 ml)
Ranchero Sauce (page 52)

4 tablespoons
(2 fl oz/60 ml) olive oil

8 corn tortillas

8 large eggs

Kosher salt and
freshly ground pepper

½ cup (2½ oz/75 g)
crumbled *queso fresco*
or feta cheese

Chopped fresh cilantro
for serving

Refried Beans (page 214)
or black beans, warmed,
for serving

MAKES 4 SERVINGS

During my college years, I spent a semester studying abroad at the University of Guadalajara in Mexico. My first breakfast with the Garcias, my host family, was an ample plate of *huevos rancheros*, complete with beans and rice, which changed my concept of breakfast forever.

1 Preheat the oven to 200°F (95°C). Have ready 4 ovenproof plates large enough to hold 2 overlapping tortillas. In a saucepan, warm the ranchero sauce over very low heat.

2 In a large frying pan, heat 2 tablespoons of the oil over high heat until the oil is shimmering. One at a time, fry the tortillas just until they begin to crisp (they should not be crunchy), about 30 seconds. Transfer to paper towels to drain. Overlap 2 tortillas on each plate and keep warm in the oven. Discard the oil in the pan.

3 Add the remaining 2 tablespoons oil to the pan and heat over medium heat. Crack 4 of the eggs into the pan. Season with salt and pepper, cover, reduce the heat to medium-low, and cook until the whites are set, about 2 minutes for sunny-side-up eggs. Or carefully flip the eggs and cook to the desired doneness. Transfer 2 eggs to each dish and keep warm in the oven while frying the remaining eggs in the same manner.

4 For each serving, spoon about ½ cup (4 fl oz/125 ml) of the warm sauce over the eggs, top with one-fourth of the *queso fresco*, and sprinkle with some cilantro. Serve at once, with the beans on the side.

HAM AND GRUYÈRE
CROQUE MADAME

4 tablespoons (2 oz/60 g)
unsalted butter

2 tablespoons
all-purpose flour

1 cup (8 fl oz/250 ml)
whole milk, warmed

1 cup (4 oz/125 g) shredded
Gruyère cheese

5 teaspoons Dijon mustard

Kosher salt and
freshly ground pepper

8 slices good-quality,
firm white sandwich bread

4 large eggs

½ lb (250 g) thinly sliced
Black Forest ham

MAKES 4 SERVINGS

A *croque madame* is so much more than a grilled ham
and cheese. In signature French fashion, this otherwise
humble sandwich is drenched in a decadent, cheesy
sauce, then broiled in the oven until bubbling and golden.
A fried egg on top is the crowning glory.

1 In a small saucepan, melt 2 tablespoons of the butter over medium-low
heat. Whisk in the flour until smooth. Let bubble without browning,
whisking frequently, for 1 minute. Gradually whisk in the warm milk,
raise the heat to medium, and bring to a gentle boil, whisking frequently.
Reduce the heat to medium-low and simmer, whisking frequently, until
thickened, about 5 minutes. Remove from the heat. Stir in ¾ cup (3 oz/
90 g) of the cheese and 1 teaspoon of the mustard. Season with salt and
pepper. Transfer to a bowl, placing a piece of plastic wrap directly onto
the surface of the sauce, and let cool.

2 Preheat the oven to 400°F (200°C). Line a rimmed baking sheet with
parchment paper. Arrange the bread slices in a single layer and bake,
turning once, until toasted on both sides, about 10 minutes. Remove
from the oven and set aside.

3 In a large frying pan, melt the remaining 2 tablespoons butter over
medium heat. Crack the eggs into the pan. Season with salt and pepper,
cover, reduce the heat to medium-low, and cook until the whites are set,
about 2 minutes for sunny-side-up eggs. Or carefully flip the eggs and
cook to the desired doneness.

4 Preheat the broiler. Spread 4 bread slices with the remaining 4 teaspoons
mustard. Add an equal amount of the sliced ham and 1 tablespoon of
the sauce to each slice. Top with the remaining bread slices. Return the
sandwiches to the prepared baking sheet. Spread the remaining sauce
over the tops of the sandwiches, and sprinkle each with 1 tablespoon
of the remaining cheese. Broil until the cheese is melted and golden,
about 2 minutes. Transfer to individual plates, top each with a fried egg,
and serve at once.

MUSHROOM OMELET
WITH FONTINA AND THYME

2 tablespoons
unsalted butter

¼ lb (125 g) white or
cremini mushrooms, sliced

¾ teaspoon minced
fresh thyme

Kosher salt and
freshly ground pepper

4 large eggs

2 tablespoons heavy cream

½ cup (2 oz/60 g)
shredded fontina cheese

MAKES 2 SERVINGS

One of my favorite weekend morning rituals is to search through the refrigerator for ingredients to fill a big, golden omelet. The earthy flavors of mushroom, thyme, and fontina make this one of the best combinations I've found. Serve with thick slices of artisan bread, brushed with extra-virgin olive oil and toasted under the broiler.

◇◇◇

1 In a frying pan, preferably nonstick, melt 1 tablespoon of the butter over medium heat. Add the mushrooms and cook, stirring occasionally, until the juices evaporate and the mushrooms begin to brown, about 6 minutes. Stir in ½ teaspoon of the thyme and season with salt and pepper. Transfer to a bowl and set aside.

2 Preheat the oven to 200°F (95°C). In a bowl, whisk together the eggs, cream, ¼ teaspoon salt, and a few grinds of pepper just until blended. Do not overbeat.

3 Add half of the remaining 1 tablespoon butter to the frying pan and melt over medium heat until hot. Tilt the pan to cover the bottom evenly with butter.

4 Add half of the egg mixture to the pan and cook until the eggs have barely begun to set around the edges, about 30 seconds. Using a heatproof spatula, lift the cooked edges and gently push them toward the center, tilting the pan to allow the liquid egg on top to flow underneath, then cook for 30 seconds. Repeat this process two more times. When the eggs are almost completely set but still slightly moist on top, sprinkle half of the cheese over half of the omelet. Scatter half of the mushrooms over the cheese.

5 Using the spatula, fold the untopped half of the omelet over the filled half to create a half-moon shape. Let the omelet cook for 30 seconds more, then slide it onto a heatproof serving plate. Keep warm in the oven. Repeat to make a second omelet in the same manner. Sprinkle both omelets with the remaining ¼ teaspoon thyme, dividing it evenly. Serve at once.

variation The nutty flavors of Gruyère or Comté cheese also work well with the mushrooms. You can also add 1 minced green onion to the mushrooms during the last minute or so of cooking.

JACK'S FIREHOUSE PHILADELPHIA, PA

Since 1989, chef Jack McDavid has been serving his "haute country" cuisine out of a converted 19th century firehouse in Philadelphia's Fairmount district. Red brick, a rich mahogany bar, and a gleaming brass fire pole pack plenty of old-world charm. In a city overflowing with American history, it is only natural that the menu is dedicated to regional fare, including New England clam chowder and an array of grilled meats such as ribs and pulled pork; wine and beer are also joined by an extensive list of whiskeys and bourbons. On Saturdays and Sundays, Jack's hauls out a serious brunch menu, which includes a version of eggs Benedict featuring filet mignon, as well as scrapple, a pork-and-cornmeal concoction that's a specialty of the Pennsylvania Dutch. The regional highlight, however, is really the cheesesteak omelet, in which Philadelphia's most popular gift to American cooking is retooled by stuffing thinly sliced beef, lots of caramelized onions and roasted peppers, and sharp aged provolone into a fluffy egg omelet instead of a hoagie roll.

PHILLY CHEESESTEAK OMELET
WITH ONIONS AND BELL PEPPERS

1 small boneless rib-eye steak, about 6 oz (185 g)

1 tablespoon unsalted butter

1 yellow onion, cut in half and sliced

3 tablespoons olive oil

1 roasted red bell pepper (page 217), peeled, seeded, and cut into thin strips

Kosher salt and freshly ground pepper

½ cup (2 oz/60 g) grated aged provolone cheese

6 large eggs

Fresh flat-leaf parsley sprigs for garnish (optional)

MAKES 2–4 SERVINGS

1 Freeze the steak until firm but not frozen, about 1 hour. Using a sharp knife, cut the steak against the grain into very thin slices. Set aside for 10–15 minutes to thaw.

2 In a frying pan, preferably nonstick, melt the butter over medium-low heat. Add the onion and cook, stirring frequently, until soft and golden brown, 15–20 minutes. Transfer to a bowl and set aside.

3 Wipe out the frying pan with paper towels. Add 1 tablespoon of the oil and heat over high heat. Add the steak slices, with as many of the flat sides touching the pan as possible. Cook until the undersides are browned, about 1 minute. Turn the steak slices, and move to one side of the pan to continue cooking. Add the onion and pepper and cook until they are reheated and the steak is medium-rare, about 30 seconds. (The mixture will continue to cook off the heat, so do not overcook.) Stir the steak, onions, and peppers to combine and season with salt and pepper. Sprinkle the cheese over the top of the steak mixture and remove the frying pan from the heat.

4 Preheat the oven to 200°F (95°C). In a bowl, whisk together the eggs, ½ teaspoon salt, and ⅛ teaspoon pepper just until thoroughly blended. Do not overbeat.

5 In a frying pan, preferably nonstick, heat 1 tablespoon of the oil over medium heat. Tilt the pan to cover the bottom evenly with oil. Add half of the egg mixture to the pan and cook until the eggs have barely begun to set around the edges, about 30 seconds. Using a heatproof spatula, lift the cooked edges and gently push them toward the center, tilting the pan to allow the liquid egg on top to flow underneath, then cook for 30 seconds. Repeat this process two more times. When the eggs are almost completely set but still slightly moist on top, transfer half of the steak mixture over half of the omelet.

6 Using the spatula, fold the untopped half of the omelet over the filled half to create a half-moon shape. Let the omelet cook for about 30 seconds more, then slide it onto a heatproof serving plate. Keep the omelet warm in the oven. Repeat to make a second omelet in the same manner.

7 Garnish each omelet with parsley sprigs, if desired. Serve the omelets warm, either whole or cut in half.

SPINACH AND BACON OMELET
WITH CHEDDAR CHEESE

4 thick slices
applewood-smoked bacon,
cut into bite-size pieces

1 tablespoon
minced shallot

4 cups (4 oz/125 g)
packed baby spinach,
rinsed but not dried

Kosher salt and
freshly ground pepper

6 large eggs

2 tablespoons
unsalted butter

1/2 cup (2 oz/60 g) shredded
sharp Cheddar cheese

Sour cream for serving
(optional)

MAKES 2–4 SERVINGS

Sautéed spinach is an excellent partner for eggs, whether scrambled, fried, or poached. It is especially delicious tucked into a big, fluffy omelet. Crispy, salty bacon and gooey, melted cheese are all the embellishments you'll need—but I'll never say no to a dollop of sour cream to gild the Lily. It's also delicious served with fresh salsa (page 213).

1 In a large frying pan, preferably nonstick, fry the bacon over medium heat until crisp and golden, about 4 minutes. Transfer to paper towels to drain. Pour off all but 2 teaspoons of the fat in the pan.

2 Add the shallot to the pan with the bacon fat and cook over medium heat, stirring often, until softened, about 1 minute. A handful at a time, add the spinach, cooking until the first batch wilts before adding another handful. Cook all of the spinach until tender, about 2 minutes. Season with salt and pepper. Drain the spinach mixture in a sieve, pressing gently to remove excess liquid. Transfer to a cutting board and coarsely chop. Set aside.

3 Preheat the oven to 200°F (95°C). In a bowl, whisk together the eggs, 2 tablespoons water, 1/4 teaspoon salt, and a few grinds of pepper just until thoroughly blended. Do not overbeat.

4 In the same frying pan, melt half of the butter over medium heat until hot. Tilt the pan to cover the bottom evenly with butter. Add half of the egg mixture and cook until the eggs have barely begun to set around the edges, about 30 seconds. Using a heatproof spatula, lift the cooked edges and gently push them toward the center, tilting the pan to allow the liquid egg on top to flow underneath, then cook for 30 seconds. Repeat this process two more times. When the eggs are almost completely set but still slightly moist on top, sprinkle half of the cheese over half of the omelet. Scatter half of the cooked bacon and half of the spinach over the cheese.

5 Using the spatula, fold the untopped half of the omelet over the filled half to create a half-moon shape. Let the omelet cook for 30 seconds more, then slide it onto a heatproof serving plate. Keep warm in the oven. Repeat to make a second omelet in the same manner. Serve at once with sour cream, if desired.

ROASTED RED PEPPER FRITTATA

WITH SAUSAGE AND FETA

2 teaspoons olive oil

6 oz (185 g) sweet Italian sausage, casing removed

8 large eggs

4 teaspoons chopped fresh basil

Kosher salt and freshly ground black pepper

1 tablespoon unsalted butter

1 roasted red bell pepper (page 217), peeled, seeded, and cut into thin strips

⅓ cup (1½ oz/45 g) crumbled feta cheese

MAKES 4 SERVINGS

The first frittata I ever ate was served in a cast iron skillet in the kitchen of my friend's grandmother. I fell in love with the Mediterranean flavors of the Italian sausage, red bell peppers, and feta cheese that she used, and have been making frittatas such as this one ever since.

1 In an ovenproof frying pan, heat the oil over medium heat. Add the sausage and cook, stirring and breaking it up with the side of a wooden spoon, until it begins to brown, about 10 minutes. Using a slotted spoon, transfer the sausage to paper towels to drain. Discard the fat in the pan.

2 Preheat the broiler. In a bowl, whisk together the eggs, 2 teaspoons of the basil, ½ teaspoon salt, and ¼ teaspoon pepper. Add the butter to the pan and melt over medium heat until hot. Return the sausage to the pan and add the roasted bell pepper. Pour the egg mixture into the sausage mixture and cook over medium heat until the edges of the frittata begin to set, about 30 seconds. Using a heatproof spatula, lift the cooked edges of the frittata, and tilt the frying pan to allow the liquid egg on top to flow underneath. Continue cooking, occasionally lifting the frittata and tilting it again, until the top is almost set, about 4 minutes more.

3 Sprinkle the top of the frittata with the cheese. Place under the broiler until the frittata puffs and becomes golden brown, about 1 minute. Sprinkle with the remaining basil. Cut into wedges and serve hot or warm.

ARTICHOKE FRITTATA
WITH POTATO AND GOAT CHEESE

1 lemon, cut in half

3 large artichokes, with stems attached

3 tablespoons olive oil

½ cup (2½ oz/75 g) finely chopped yellow onion

1 large russet potato, peeled and thinly sliced

Kosher salt and freshly ground pepper

8 large eggs

1½ teaspoons minced fresh oregano

⅓ cup (1½ oz/45 g) crumbled fresh goat cheese

MAKES 4 SERVINGS

During my California childhood, we would often buy artichokes at roadside farmstands, then steam them and turn the freshly cooked artichoke hearts into plump frittatas. Trimming artichokes takes practice, but is worth the effort: frozen artichoke hearts just don't compare.

1 Squeeze the juice of ½ lemon into a bowl and add 1 quart (32 fl oz/1 l) cold water and the spent lemon half. Working with one artichoke at a time, snap off the tough, dark green leaves until you reveal a cone of tender pale green leaves. Cut off the stem at the base. Rub the cut areas with the remaining lemon half. Using the tip of a paring knife, trim away the thick skin from each stem, and add the stems to the lemon water. Cut off the leaves where they meet the base and discard the leaves. Cut out and discard the fuzzy choke. Rub the heart all over with the lemon half, then add to the lemon water along with the second lemon half.

2 Drain the artichoke hearts and stems in a sieve and rinse under cold running water. Cut the stems in half lengthwise. Thinly slice the artichoke hearts. In an ovenproof frying pan, heat 1 tablespoon of the oil over medium heat. Add the artichoke hearts and stems and cook, stirring occasionally, until the edges begin to brown, about 5 minutes. Add the onion and cook until softened, about 2 minutes. Add ¼ cup (2 fl oz/60 ml) water and cover. Reduce the heat to medium-low. Cook until the artichoke pieces are tender when pierced with the tip of a knife and the liquid has evaporated, about 20 minutes. Transfer to a bowl and set aside.

3 In the same frying pan, heat the remaining 2 tablespoons oil over medium heat. Add the potato and turn to coat with the oil. Cover and cook, stirring occasionally, until tender, about 5 minutes. Stir in the artichoke mixture. Season lightly with salt and pepper.

4 Preheat the broiler. In a bowl, whisk together the eggs, 1 teaspoon of the oregano, ¾ teaspoon salt, and ¼ teaspoon pepper. Pour the egg mixture into the potato mixture and cook over medium heat until the edges begin to set. Using a heatproof spatula, lift the cooked edges of the frittata, and tilt the frying pan to allow the liquid egg on top to flow underneath. Continue cooking the frittata, occasionally lifting and tilting it, until the top is almost set, about 4 minutes more.

5 Sprinkle the top of the frittata with the cheese. Place under the broiler until the frittata puffs and becomes golden brown, about 1 minute. Sprinkle with the remaining ½ teaspoon oregano. Cut into wedges and serve hot or warm.

POACHED EGGS

WITH CREAMY POLENTA AND PECORINO

1 cup (8 fl oz/250 ml)
whole milk

Kosher salt and
freshly ground pepper

1 cup (7 oz/220 g)
coarse-ground polenta

¼ lb (125 g) sliced pancetta

2 tablespoons
distilled white vinegar

4 large eggs

¾ cup (3 oz/90 g) grated
pecorino cheese,
plus cheese shavings
for garnish

2 teaspoons minced
fresh rosemary or thyme,
plus more for garnish

MAKES 4 SERVINGS

Rich, nutty cheese stirred into creamy polenta and topped with a poached egg just might be the most comforting breakfast imaginable. For the fullest flavor and texture, use coarsely ground polenta, rather than instant. I like to use a mellow aged sheep's milk cheese, such as Italian *pecorino toscano* or Spanish Manchego.

◇◇◇

1 In a large, heavy saucepan, bring 3 cups (24 fl oz/750 ml) water, the milk, and 1 teaspoon salt to a boil over medium-high heat. Gradually whisk in the polenta. Reduce the heat to medium-low and cover. Cook, whisking frequently, until the polenta is thick and creamy, about 45 minutes. Add up to ½ cup (4 fl oz/125 ml) water by tablespoons if the polenta begins to stick to the bottom of the pan. (Be careful as the hot polenta can splatter.) Season with pepper.

2 In a frying pan, cook the pancetta over medium heat, turning once, until crisped and browned, about 7 minutes. Transfer to paper towels to drain. Coarsely chop and set aside.

3 In a wide saucepan, combine 8 cups (64 fl oz/2 l) water and the vinegar and bring to a boil over high heat. Reduce the heat to medium-low to keep the water at a simmer. Fill a bowl halfway with hot tap water and place it near the stove.

4 Crack an egg into a small bowl. Slip the egg from the bowl into the simmering water. Using a large metal spoon, quickly spoon the egg white back toward the center of the egg to help the egg set in an oval shape. Simmer gently until the egg white is opaque and the egg is just firm enough to hold its shape, 3–4 minutes. Using a large slotted spoon, lift the egg out of the simmering water. Trim off any floppy bits of white and carefully transfer the egg to the bowl of hot water. Repeat to poach the remaining eggs.

5 Add the grated cheese, 2 teaspoons rosemary, and the chopped pancetta to the polenta and stir to combine. Spoon equal amounts of the polenta into 4 soup bowls. One at a time, using a slotted spoon, remove the poached eggs from the hot water, resting the bottom of the spoon briefly on a clean kitchen towel to blot excess moisture, and place an egg on each serving. Top with some cheese shavings, a sprinkling of rosemary, and a few grinds of pepper. Serve at once.

EGGS BLACKSTONE
WITH ROASTED TOMATOES

4 plum tomatoes,
cut in half lengthwise

1 tablespoon olive oil,
plus more for cooking

1 teaspoon minced
fresh thyme

Kosher salt and freshly
ground pepper

8 slices thick-cut
applewood-smoked bacon,
halved crosswise

4 English muffins,
split crosswise

2 tablespoons
distilled white vinegar

8 large eggs

About 1 cup (8 fl oz/250 ml)
Portage Bay Cafe's
Hollandaise Sauce
(page 212)

MAKES 4 SERVINGS

Poached eggs and hollandaise sauce are a decadent combination with many celebrated variations. Eggs Benedict is perhaps the best known, but Eggs Blackstone, a personal favorite, substitutes crisp bacon and tomatoes for the Canadian bacon. For the fullest flavor, I like to roast the tomatoes, drizzled first with olive oil and sprinkled with fresh thyme.

1 Preheat the oven to 400°F (200°C). Lightly oil a rimmed baking sheet. Arrange the tomatoes, cut side up, on the baking sheet. Drizzle with the 1 tablespoon oil, then sprinkle with the thyme, ½ teaspoon salt, and ¼ teaspoon pepper. Bake until the tomatoes have shrunk slightly and their juices are bubbling, about 30 minutes.

2 In a large frying pan, fry the bacon over medium heat, turning once, until crisp and browned, about 6 minutes. Transfer to paper towels to drain. Meanwhile, preheat the broiler. Place the muffins, cut side up, on a baking sheet and toast in the broiler until lightly crisped, about 1 minute. Remove from the broiler and set aside.

3 In a wide saucepan, combine 8 cups (64 fl oz/2 l) water and the vinegar and bring to a boil over high heat. Reduce the heat to medium-low to keep the water at a simmer. Fill a bowl halfway with hot tap water and place it near the stove.

4 Crack an egg into a small bowl. Slip the egg from the bowl into the simmering water. Using a large metal spoon, quickly spoon the egg white back toward the center of the egg to help the egg set in an oval shape. Simmer gently until the egg white is opaque and the egg is just firm enough to hold its shape, 3–4 minutes. Using a large slotted spoon, lift the egg out of the simmering water. Trim off any floppy bits of white and carefully transfer the egg to the bowl of hot water. Repeat to poach the remaining eggs.

5 To serve, place 2 muffin halves, cut side up, on each plate. Top each half with 2 pieces of bacon and 1 roasted tomato half. One at a time, using a slotted spoon, remove the poached eggs from the water, resting the bottom of the spoon briefly on a clean kitchen towel to blot excess moisture, and perch an egg on each muffin half. Spoon about 3 tablespoons of hollandaise over each serving, then sprinkle with pepper. Serve at once, passing the remaining hollandaise sauce on the side.

PORTAGE BAY CAFE SEATTLE, WA

Portage Bay Cafe owners John and Amy Fair Gunnar put their culinary philosophy into action by sourcing as much of their food as possible from local suppliers, including organic coffees, artisanal cheeses, handmade breads, and natural meats. The ingredient-driven menu has resonated with Seattle residents, who enjoy breakfast and lunch at three popular locations. Hot-from-the griddle pancakes and French toast invite a trip to the toppings bar, where guests can load up on as much fruit, nuts, and pure maple syrup as they can fit on their plates. The attention to local foods extends to the region's famed seafood, spotlighted in dishes such as a house-smoked wild salmon omelet and the crab cake Benedict. Dungeness crabs, a particular pride of the Pacific Northwest, are often eaten freshly cracked with lemon and butter, making hollandaise sauce a logical—and absolutely delicious—leap for the brunch plate. The crunchy crab cake makes a great stand-in for the toasted English muffin you'd find in a classic Benedict.

CRAB CAKE EGGS BENEDICT
WITH SAUTÉED SPINACH

⅓ cup (3 fl oz/80 ml)
mayonnaise

3 green onions, white and
green parts, minced

⅓ cup (2 oz/60 g)
minced yellow onion

¼ cup (1 oz/30 g)
finely grated carrot

3 tablespoons peeled
and grated fresh ginger

2 tablespoons sesame
seeds, toasted (page 217)

2 teaspoons
fresh lemon juice

12 oz (375 g) fresh-cooked
lump crabmeat,
preferably Dungeness

1 cup (1½ oz/45 g) panko,
or as needed

Kosher salt and
freshly ground pepper

1 tablespoon
unsalted butter

12 oz (375 g) baby spinach,
rinsed but not dried

2 tablespoons canola oil

2 tablespoons distilled
white vinegar

8 large eggs

About 1 cup (8 fl oz/250 ml)
Portage Bay Cafe's
Hollandaise Sauce
(page 212)

MAKES 4–8 SERVINGS

1 To prepare the crab cakes, line a baking sheet with parchment paper. In a bowl, mix together the mayonnaise, green onions, yellow onion, carrot, ginger, sesame seeds, and lemon juice. Pick over the crabmeat for shell shards and cartilage. Add to the mayonnaise mixture and mix gently until combined. Stir in about ½ cup (¾ oz/20 g) panko, just enough to let the mixture hold its shape when formed into a cake. (The exact amount depends on the moisture content of the crab.) Season to taste with salt and pepper.

2 Divide the mixture into 8 equal portions and shape each portion into a thick cake. Spread the remaining ½ cup panko in a shallow dish. Coat the cakes evenly with the panko, and transfer to the prepared baking sheet. Refrigerate for at least 15 minutes or up to 1 hour.

3 In a large saucepan, melt the butter over medium heat. A handful at a time, add the spinach, cooking until the batch wilts before adding another handful. Cook all of the spinach until just wilted, about 1 minute. Drain the spinach in a sieve, pressing gently to remove some, but not all, excess liquid. Season the spinach with salt and pepper. Return to the saucepan and keep warm over very low heat.

4 Line another rimmed baking sheet with paper towels. In a large frying pan, heat the oil over medium heat until it shimmers. Add the crab cakes and cook until the undersides are golden brown, 2–3 minutes. Flip the cakes and cook until the other sides are golden brown, 2–3 minutes more. Using a slotted spatula, transfer to the paper towels to drain briefly.

5 In a wide saucepan, combine 8 cups (64 fl oz/2 l) water and the vinegar and bring to a boil over high heat. Reduce the heat to medium-low to keep the water at a simmer. Fill a bowl halfway with hot tap water and place it near the stove.

6 Crack an egg into a small bowl. Slip the egg from the bowl into the simmering water. Using a large metal spoon, quickly spoon the egg white back toward the center of the egg to help the egg set in an oval shape. Simmer gently until the egg white is opaque and the egg is just firm enough to hold its shape, 3–4 minutes. Using a large slotted spoon, lift the egg out of the simmering water. Trim off any floppy bits of white and carefully transfer the egg to the bowl of hot water. Repeat to poach the remaining eggs.

7 To serve, place 1 or 2 crab cakes on each plate. Using tongs, top each cake with a mound of spinach. One at a time, using a slotted spoon, remove the poached eggs from the water, resting the bottom of the spoon briefly on a clean kitchen towel to blot excess moisture, and perch an egg on each cake. Spoon 1–2 tablespoons of hollandaise over each egg. Serve at once, passing the remaining sauce on the side.

CORN AND CHILE STRATA

WITH MEXICAN CHORIZO

3 poblano chiles

1½ cups (9 oz/280 g) fresh or thawed frozen corn kernels

1 tablespoon olive oil, plus more for cooking

1 lb (500 g) fresh Mexican-style chorizo sausage, casings removed

1 white onion, chopped

2 cups (16 fl oz/500 ml) whole milk

8 large eggs

½ teaspoon hot pepper sauce

Kosher salt

12 slices day-old baguette, each ½–¾ inch (12 mm–2 cm) thick

2 cups (8 oz/250 g) shredded Cheddar cheese

MAKES 8–10 SERVINGS

Strata, a casserole of eggs, bread, cheese, and other ingredients, is a busy cook's secret weapon: The dish can be assembled the night before, then baked the next morning to golden perfection. Use fresh Mexican-style chorizo, not smoked Spanish sausage links, for this southwestern version, which is studded with mild green chiles and sweet corn.

1 Preheat the broiler. Place the chiles on a baking sheet and broil, turning occasionally, until blackened on all sides, about 12 minutes. Transfer to a cutting board and let cool until easy to handle. Peel off the blackened skin. Discard the stem, seeds, and ribs, and chop the chiles. Transfer to a bowl and add the corn.

2 Meanwhile, in a large frying pan, heat the 1 tablespoon oil over medium heat. Add the chorizo and cook, breaking it up with the side of a wooden spoon, until it begins to brown, about 8 minutes. Add the onion and cook, stirring occasionally, until the onion softens, about 3 minutes more. Using a slotted spoon, transfer the sausage mixture to paper towels to drain. Discard the fat in the pan.

3 Lightly oil a 3-quart (3-l) baking dish. In a large bowl, whisk together the milk, eggs, hot pepper sauce, and ¾ teaspoon salt until combined. Arrange 6 of the bread slices in a single layer on the bottom of the prepared dish, tearing the slices to fit, if needed. Top evenly with half of the chorizo mixture, half of the chile mixture, and half of the cheese. Repeat with the remaining bread slices, chorizo and chile mixtures, and cheese.

4 Slowly pour the milk mixture over the layers. Wrap securely in plastic wrap. Press gently on the plastic to submerge the layers in the milk mixture. Refrigerate for at least 2 hours or up to overnight.

5 Preheat the oven to 350°F (180°C). Uncover and bake until the strata puffs and becomes golden brown, about 1 hour. Transfer to a wire rack and let cool for 5 minutes. Serve warm.

BAKED EGGS

WITH SPINACH AND PROSCIUTTO

1 tablespoon
unsalted butter

1½ lb (750 g) spinach,
rinsed but not dried

1 teaspoon olive oil

3 oz (90 g) prosciutto,
chopped

¾ cup (6 fl oz/180 ml) plus
4 teaspoons heavy cream

Kosher salt and
freshly ground pepper

A few gratings of
fresh nutmeg

4 large eggs

4 teaspoons freshly grated
Parmesan cheese

MAKES 4 SERVINGS

Here, I bake eggs in a nest of spinach, prosciutto, and cream for a presentation that is elegant enough for brunch entertaining. For the soft-cooked egg lover, it's a heavenly combination; make sure to provide toasted bread or English muffins for dipping into the buttery yolks.

1 Preheat the oven to 350°F (180°C). Butter four ¾-cup (6-fl oz/180-ml) ramekins, and set aside.

2 In a large saucepan, melt the 1 tablespoon butter over medium heat. A handful at a time, add the spinach, cooking until the first batch wilts before adding another handful. Cook all of the spinach until tender, about 3 minutes. Drain the spinach in a sieve, pressing gently to remove excess liquid. Transfer to a chopping board and coarsely chop.

3 Heat the oil in the saucepan over medium heat. Add the prosciutto and cook, stirring occasionally, until its fat softens, about 2 minutes. Add the spinach and the ¾ cup cream and bring to a boil. Cook, stirring often, until the cream has thickened and reduced to a few tablespoons, about 4 minutes. Season with salt, pepper, and nutmeg. Divide evenly among the prepared ramekins. Break an egg into each ramekin. Season the top of each with salt and pepper, and drizzle each with 1 teaspoon of the cream. Carefully arrange the ramekins on a rimmed baking sheet.

4 Bake, watching the eggs carefully to avoid overcooking, until the whites are opaque and the yolks have firm edges and are soft in the center, about 15 minutes. Remove from the oven and sprinkle each serving with 1 teaspoon of the Parmesan. Serve at once.

BROCCOLI-CHEDDAR QUICHE

Buttery Pastry Dough
(page 215)

Flour for rolling out
the dough

2 cups (4 oz/125 g)
broccoli florets

1 cup (8 fl oz/250 ml)
half-and-half

2 large eggs

1 tablespoon minced
fresh dill

Kosher salt and
freshly ground pepper

1 cup (4 oz/125 g) shredded
sharp Cheddar cheese

MAKES 6 SERVINGS

Quiche has come in and out of style over the years, but in my opinion, it remains the ultimate brunch dish. A buttery, flaky pastry crust is irresistible, and the possibilities for fillings are endless. Broccoli and Cheddar are a universally appealing combination, and I've found this to be one of my most popular versions.

1 Place the dough on a lightly floured work surface and dust the top with flour. (If the dough is chilled hard, let it stand at room temperature for a few minutes until it begins to soften before rolling it out.) Roll out into a round about 12 inches (30 cm) in diameter and about ⅛ inch (3 mm) thick. Transfer to a 9-inch (23-cm) tart pan with a removable bottom, gently fitting the dough into the bottom and sides of the pan. Using scissors or a small knife, trim the dough, leaving a ½-inch (12-mm) overhang. Fold the overhanging dough over and into the pan, pressing it firmly against the sides of the pan; the dough should be doubly thick at the sides and rise about ⅛ inch (3 mm) above the sides of the pan rim. Pierce the dough all over with a fork. Line the dough with aluminum foil and freeze for 15–30 minutes.

2 Position a rack in the lower third of the oven and preheat to 375°F (190°C). Place the dough-lined pan on a baking sheet and fill the foil with pie weights or dried beans. Bake until the dough is set and beginning to brown, about 20 minutes.

3 Meanwhile, make the filling. Bring a medium saucepan three-fourths full of lightly salted water to a boil over high heat. Add the broccoli and cook until the florets are barely tender, about 5 minutes. Drain well, and pat dry with kitchen towels. In a bowl, whisk together the half-and-half, eggs, dill, ½ teaspoon salt, and ¼ teaspoon pepper until combined.

4 Remove the baking sheet with the tart pan from the oven. Remove the foil and weights. Scatter the broccoli and cheese evenly in the pastry shell. Carefully pour the egg mixture into the shell. Return the sheet to the oven and reduce the oven temperature to 350°F (180°C). Bake until the filling is puffed and golden brown, about 35 minutes. Let cool slightly, then serve.

variation Instead of the broccoli, use trimmed asparagus spears, cut into 1-inch (2.5-cm) lengths and blanched in boiling water until tender-crisp, about 3 minutes. You may also wish to substitute Gruyère for the Cheddar cheese.

HAM AND CHEESE QUICHE
WITH CRÈME FRAÎCHE AND CHIVES

Buttery Pastry Dough
(page 215)

Flour for rolling out
the dough

1 cup (8 oz/250 g)
crème fraîche

2 large eggs

1 tablespoon minced
fresh chives

2 teaspoons Dijon mustard

Kosher salt and
freshly ground pepper

6 oz (185 g) smoked ham,
cubed

¾ cup (3 oz/90 g)
shredded Gruyère cheese

MAKES 6 SERVINGS

Smoked ham and Gruyère cheese are classic ingredients in this celebrated French dish. My version adds a touch of crème fraîche for flavor and richness and a sprinkle of chives for freshness. Quiche is equally delicious served warm or at room temperature, which makes it ideal for almost any occasion.

◇◇◇

1 Place the dough on a lightly floured work surface and dust the top with flour. (If the dough is chilled hard, let it stand at room temperature for a few minutes until it begins to soften before rolling it out.) Roll out into a round about 12 inches (30 cm) in diameter and about ⅛ inch (3 mm) thick. Transfer to a 9-inch (23-cm) tart pan with a removable bottom, gently fitting the dough into the bottom and sides of the pan. Using scissors or a small knife, trim the dough, leaving a ½-inch (12-mm) overhang. Fold the overhanging dough over and into the pan, pressing it firmly against the sides of the pan; the dough should be doubly thick at the sides and rise about ⅛ inch (3 mm) above the sides of the pan rim. Pierce the dough all over with a fork. Line the dough with aluminum foil and freeze for 15–30 minutes.

2 Position a rack in the lower third of the oven and preheat to 375°F (190°C). Place the dough-lined pan on a baking sheet and fill the foil with pie weights or dried beans. Bake until the dough is set and beginning to brown, about 20 minutes.

3 Meanwhile, make the filling. In a bowl, whisk together the crème fraîche, eggs, chives, mustard, ½ teaspoon salt, and ¼ teaspoon pepper until combined.

4 Remove the baking sheet with the tart pan from the oven. Remove the foil and weights. Scatter the ham and cheese evenly in the pastry shell. Carefully pour the egg mixture into the shell. Return the sheet to the oven and reduce the oven temperature to 350°F (180°C). Bake until the filling is puffed and golden brown, about 35 minutes. Let cool slightly, then serve.

variation Instead of the ham, substitute 4 bacon strips, coarsely chopped, then cooked until crisp and browned, about 4 minutes.

3

SWEET TREATS

BLUEBERRY MUFFINS

WITH ALMOND STREUSEL

2 cups (10 oz/315 g)
all-purpose flour

²/₃ cup (5 oz/155 g) sugar

½ teaspoon baking powder

½ teaspoon baking soda

¼ teaspoon fine sea salt

1 cup (8 fl oz/250 ml)
buttermilk

2 large eggs

5 tablespoons (2½ oz/75 g)
unsalted butter,
melted and cooled

½ teaspoon
pure vanilla extract

¼ teaspoon almond
extract (optional)

1½ cups (6 oz/185 g)
fresh or frozen blueberries

Almond Streusel
¼ cup (1½ oz/45 g)
all-purpose flour

2 tablespoons sugar

2 tablespoons unsalted
butter, at room temperature

⅓ cup (1½ oz/45 g)
sliced almonds

MAKES 12 MUFFINS

A buttery, crunchy almond streusel tops these traditional blueberry muffins. Of course, they are perfect in summer, when fresh plump blueberries are at their peak, but you can substitute frozen blueberries other times of the year; remember to extend the baking time by a few extra minutes, to compensate for the colder batter.

1 Preheat the oven to 400°F (200°C). Butter and flour 12 standard muffin cups or line them with paper liners. Butter the top of the muffin pan.

2 In a bowl, sift together the flour, sugar, baking powder, baking soda, and salt. In another bowl, whisk together the buttermilk, eggs, melted butter, vanilla, and almond extract, if using. Pour the buttermilk mixture over the flour mixture and stir together just until combined. Fold in the blueberries. Divide the batter evenly among the muffin cups.

3 To make the streusel, in a small bowl, combine the flour, sugar, and butter. Using your fingers, work the ingredients together just until combined. Work in the almonds. Press together into a ball, and then separate with your fingers into coarse crumbs. Sprinkle the almond streusel evenly over the tops of the muffins.

4 Bake until the muffins are golden brown and a toothpick inserted into the center of a muffin comes out almost clean, 20–25 minutes. Transfer to a wire rack and let cool in the pan for 15 minutes, then turn out onto the rack. Serve warm or at room temperature.

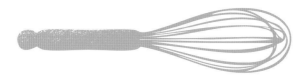

GINGER-APRICOT MUFFINS

2¼ cups (11½ oz/360 g) all-purpose flour

1 cup (8 oz/250 g) granulated sugar

1 tablespoon baking powder

¼ teaspoon fine sea salt

⅔ cup (5 fl oz/160 ml) canola oil

½ cup (4 fl oz/125 ml) whole milk

2 large eggs

⅓ cup (3 fl oz/80 ml) canned apricot nectar

½ cup (3 oz/90 g) finely chopped crystallized ginger

¼–½ cup (2½–5 oz/75–155 g) apricot preserves

2 tablespoons coarse sugar, such as turbinado

MAKES 12 MUFFINS

Ginger is one of my favorite flavor pairings with apricots; here, tiny pieces of spicy, crystallized ginger are studded throughout a moist, apricot-flavored batter. Enjoy these easy-to-make yet elegant treats at your next brunch party—the pockets of sticky preserves hidden in the muffin centers are always a fun surprise.

◇◇

1 Preheat the oven to 400°F (200°C). Butter and flour 12 standard muffin cups or line them with paper liners. Butter the top of the muffin pan.

2 In a bowl, sift together the flour, sugar, baking powder, and salt. In another bowl, whisk together the oil, milk, eggs, and apricot nectar. Pour the milk mixture over the flour mixture and stir together just until combined. Fold in the crystallized ginger.

3 Spoon half of the batter evenly among the muffin cups. Spoon 1–2 teaspoons of the apricot preserves into each cup, taking care that the preserves do not touch the side of the cup. Top with the remaining batter, covering the preserves. Sprinkle the tops with the coarse sugar, dividing it evenly.

4 Bake until the muffins are golden brown and spring back when pressed lightly with your fingertips, about 20 minutes. Transfer to a wire rack and let cool in the pan for 15 minutes. Invert onto the rack and let cool slightly before serving.

variation To make glazed muffins, omit the coarse sugar. While the muffins are baking, in a small saucepan, stir together 2 tablespoons apricot preserves and 1 tablespoon water or apricot liqueur. Bring to a boil over medium-low heat, stirring frequently with a heatproof spatula. Simmer until slightly thickened, about 1 minute. Using the spatula, spread the preserves over the top of each baked muffin. Let cool for 5 minutes more before serving.

CREAM-CURRANT SCONES
WITH QUICK STRAWBERRY JAM

Quick Strawberry Jam

1 quart (1 lb/500 g)
strawberries, stemmed,
cored, and sliced

1 cup (8 oz/250 g) sugar

2 tablespoons
fresh lemon juice

Scones

2 cups (10 oz/315 g)
all-purpose flour

3 tablespoons sugar

2½ teaspoons
baking powder

¼ teaspoon fine sea salt

½ cup (4 oz/125 g)
unsalted butter,
cut into tablespoons,
chilled, plus room
temperature butter
for serving

½ cup (3 oz/90 g)
dried currants

1 cup (8 fl oz/250 ml)
heavy cream

MAKES 8 SCONES

Tender, currant-studded scones are made all the more decadent when slathered with fresh homemade jam. This small-batch recipe for sweet strawberry jam does not require any arduous canning, as long as it is kept refrigerated and eaten within a few weeks. With scones like these around, I guarantee that finishing the jam will not be a problem.

1 To make the jam, place a saucer in the freezer to chill. Have ready a small stainless steel bowl set in a larger bowl of ice water. In a saucepan, combine the strawberries, sugar, and lemon juice. Bring to a boil over medium heat, stirring constantly to dissolve the sugar. Reduce the heat to medium-low and cook, uncovered, stirring occasionally, until the berries are tender and the juices thicken, about 10 minutes. To test, remove the chilled saucer from the freezer. Spoon about 1 teaspoon of the strawberry liquid onto the saucer and let stand for 15 seconds. If the liquid thickens to a jamlike consistency, then the jam is ready. If not, cook for a minute or two longer. Transfer to the reserved stainless steel bowl set in the bowl of ice water and let stand until cooled and thickened.

2 Meanwhile, make the scones. Preheat the oven to 400°F (200°C). Line a baking sheet with parchment paper.

3 In a bowl, sift together the flour, sugar, baking powder, and salt. Using a pastry blender or 2 knives, cut the ½ cup butter into the flour mixture just until the mixture forms coarse crumbs about the size of peas. Stir in the currants. Pour the cream over the dry ingredients and stir with a fork or rubber spatula just until combined.

4 Turn the dough out onto a lightly floured work surface. Using floured hands, pat out into a round about ½ inch (12 mm) thick. Using a 3-inch (7.5-cm) biscuit cutter, cut out as many rounds of the dough as possible. Gather up the scraps, knead briefly, and continue patting and cutting out to make 8 scones. Place 1 inch (2.5 cm) apart on the prepared baking sheet.

5 Bake until golden brown, 17–20 minutes. Transfer to a wire rack and let cool slightly. Serve warm or at room temperature, with the strawberry jam and butter on the side.

MICHAEL'S GENUINE FOOD & DRINK MIAMI, FL

Michael Schwartz, chef-owner of Michael's Genuine Food & Drink, set out to create an unpretentious but uncompromisingly fresh and delicious neighborhood eatery. Miami was the first beneficiary of his vision, and he has since opened a second location in Grand Cayman. The extraordinary brunch menu has French influences such as confit, rillettes, and brioche, as well as some more multicultural dishes that spiral towards whimsical, such as a kimchi Benedict, a rice cake filled with chorizo, and a snack of crispy pig ears. Feeling less adventurous? Pastry chef Hedy Goldsmith doesn't shy away from playing up childhood favorites, delighting patrons with upscale versions of all-American breakfast icons such as doughnuts and even homemade pop-tarts. A delicious example is her riff on a traditional scone, which includes decadent chunks of white chocolate in the buttery pastry, and a side of tart-sweet Meyer lemon curd. For the best results, Goldsmith recommends using white chocolate made from cocoa butter.

WHITE CHOCOLATE SCONES
WITH MEYER LEMON CURD

2⅓ cups (12 oz/375 g)
all-purpose flour

2 tablespoons
granulated sugar

1 tablespoon
baking powder

¼ teaspoon freshly
grated nutmeg

¼ teaspoon fine sea salt

13 tablespoons
(6½ oz/200 g) unsalted
butter, cut into cubes,
chilled

¾ cup (4 oz/125 g)
white chocolate chunks

⅓ cup (3 fl oz/80 ml)
half-and-half

2 large eggs plus
1 large egg yolk

½ teaspoon pure
vanilla extract

Meyer Lemon Curd
6–7 Meyer lemons

3 large eggs plus
4 large egg yolks

¾ cup (6 oz/185 g)
granulated sugar

½ cup (4 oz/125 g)
unsalted butter,
cut into tablespoons,
at room temperature

1 large egg beaten with
1 tablespoon whole milk,
for brushing

1 tablespoon
turbinado sugar

MAKES 12 SCONES

1 To make the scones, start the night before baking. (This allows time to chill the butter in the dough to guarantee a flaky scone.) In a bowl, sift together the flour, granulated sugar, baking powder, nutmeg, and salt. Using a pastry blender or 2 knives, cut the butter into the flour mixture just until the mixture forms coarse crumbs about the size of peas. Stir in the white chocolate. In another bowl, whisk together the half-and-half, the 2 eggs and 1 egg yolk, and vanilla. Pour the half-and-half mixture over the dry ingredients and stir with a fork or rubber spatula just until combined.

2 Turn the dough out onto a large sheet of parchment paper dusted with flour. Roll out the dough into a rectangle about 1 inch (2.5 cm) thick. Transfer the dough and the parchment paper to a rimmed baking sheet. Cover tightly with plastic wrap and refrigerate at least 6 hours or up to 3 days.

3 To make the lemon curd, finely grate the zest from 2 lemons. Juice enough lemons to make ⅔ cup (5 fl oz/160 ml) juice. In the bottom part of a double boiler, bring 1 inch (2.5 cm) of water to a boil over high heat. Reduce the heat to low to maintain a simmer. Set a wire sieve in a bowl near the stove.

4 In the top part of the double boiler, whisk together the lemon juice and zest, the 3 eggs, 4 egg yolks, and granulated sugar. Place over (not touching) the simmering water. Using a heatproof spatula, stir the lemon mixture constantly, scraping down any splashes from the sides, and cook until it is thick enough to coat the spatula, about 5 minutes. Strain through the sieve into the bowl. One tablespoon at a time, whisk in the butter. Let cool to room temperature. Press a piece of plastic wrap directly onto the surface of the lemon curd and refrigerate until chilled and firmer, at least 4 hours. (The lemon curd can be made up to 3 days ahead.)

5 Preheat the oven to 375°F (190°C). Line another baking sheet with parchment paper. Remove the dough on the baking sheet from the refrigerator. Using a 2½-inch (6-cm) biscuit cutter, cut out as many rounds of dough as possible. Gather up the scraps, gently press together, and continue patting and cutting out to make 12 scones. Place about 1 inch (2.5 cm) apart on the prepared baking sheet. Lightly brush the tops of the scones with some of the egg-milk mixture, and sprinkle with equal amounts of the turbinado sugar.

6 Bake until golden brown, 17–20 minutes. Transfer to a wire rack and let cool slightly. Serve warm or at room temperature, with the lemon curd on the side.

BLACKBERRY COFFEE CAKE
WITH PECAN STREUSEL

2 cups (10 oz/315 g)
plus 1 tablespoon
all-purpose flour

1/2 teaspoon *each*
baking powder, baking
soda, and fine sea salt

1 cup (8 oz/250 g)
unsalted butter,
at room temperature

1 3/4 cups (14 oz/440 g)
granulated sugar

Finely grated zest
of 1 orange

2 large eggs, beaten,
at room temperature

1 teaspoon
pure vanilla extract

1 cup (8 oz/250 g)
sour cream, at room
temperature

1 pint (8 oz/250 g)
blackberries

2 tablespoons firmly
packed light brown sugar

1 teaspoon
ground cinnamon

Pecan Streusel
3/4 cup (4 oz/125 g)
all-purpose flour

1/3 cup (2 1/2 oz/75 g)
firmly packed
light brown sugar

6 tablespoons (3 oz/90 g)
unsalted butter,
at room temperature

1 cup (4 oz/125 g) coarsely
chopped pecans

MAKES 12 SERVINGS

Wild blackberries grew profusely in vacant lots throughout my California home town. My brothers and I deftly avoided the sharp brambles to snatch the juicy fruit, emerging with a cache of berries and darkly stained hands. A moist, streusel-topped coffee cake is the perfect canvas for blackberries, creating a quintessential midsummer breakfast treat.

1 Preheat the oven to 350°F (180°C). Lightly butter a 9-by-13-inch (23-by-33-cm) baking dish. Dust the pan with a little flour, tapping out the excess.

2 In a bowl, sift together the 2 cups flour, the baking powder, baking soda, and salt. In another bowl, using a handheld mixer on high speed, beat together the butter, granulated sugar, and orange zest until light in color and texture, about 3 minutes. Gradually beat in the eggs, and then the vanilla. Reduce the speed to low and add the flour mixture in 3 additions alternately with the sour cream in 2 additions, beginning and ending with the flour mixture and stopping to scrape down the bowl as needed, beating until smooth.

3 In a third bowl, combine the blackberries with the brown sugar, cinnamon, and the 1 tablespoon flour. Spread half of the batter in the prepared pan. Top with the berry mixture, taking care that no berries touch the sides of the pan. Spread the remaining batter over the berries, smoothing the top.

4 To make the streusel, in a small bowl, combine the flour, brown sugar, and room-temperature butter. Using your fingers, work the ingredients together just until combined. Work in the pecans. Press together into a ball, and then separate with your fingers into coarse crumbs. Sprinkle the streusel evenly over the cake.

5 Bake until a wooden toothpick inserted in the center of the cake comes out clean, about 45 minutes. Transfer to a wire rack and let cool in the pan for 15 minutes. Cut the cake into squares and serve.

APPLESAUCE AND BROWN SUGAR
CRUMB CAKE

3 cups (15 oz/470 g)
all-purpose flour

1 teaspoon baking soda

1 teaspoon
ground cinnamon

¼ teaspoon fine sea salt

1 cup (8 oz/250 g)
granulated sugar

1 cup (7 oz/220 g) firmly
packed light brown sugar

¾ cup (6 fl oz/180 ml)
vegetable oil

¾ cup (7 oz/220 g)
unsweetened applesauce

3 large eggs

3 Golden Delicious or
Empire apples, peeled,
cored, and cut into cubes
(about 6 cups/1½ lb/750 g)

Streusel
1 cup (5 oz/155 g)
all-purpose flour

½ cup (4 oz/125 g)
unsalted butter,
cut into tablespoons,
at room temperature

½ cup (3½ oz/105 g) firmly
packed light brown sugar

MAKES 12 SERVINGS

This old-fashioned, rather humble cake reminds me of the best offering from a neighborhood bake sale. Chunks of apples stud the cinnamon-scented cake, and a thick layer of brown sugar streusel crumbles with every bite. Cut it into big slabs and eat it out of hand for the most fun.

1 Preheat the oven to 350°F (180°C). Lightly butter a 9-by-13-inch (23-by-33-cm) baking pan. Dust the pan with a little flour, tapping out the excess.

2 In a bowl, sift together the flour, baking soda, cinnamon, and salt. In another bowl, whisk together both sugars, the oil, the applesauce, and eggs. Make a well in the flour mixture and add the applesauce mixture. Stir with a wooden spoon just until smooth. Add the chopped apples and stir until combined. Spread the batter in the prepared pan, smoothing the top.

3 To make the streusel, in a bowl, combine the flour, butter, and brown sugar. Using your fingers, work the ingredients together just until combined. Press together into a ball, and then separate with your fingers into coarse crumbs. Sprinkle the streusel evenly over the top of the cake.

4 Bake until a toothpick inserted in the center of the cake comes out clean, about 1 hour. Transfer to a wire rack and let cool completely in the pan. Cut into squares and serve at room temperature.

variation Add ½ cup (2 oz/60 g) chopped toasted walnuts (page 217) to the batter.

MINDY SEGAL'S
ORANGE BRIOCHE ROLLS

1/3 cup (3 fl oz/80 ml) plus
1 tablespoon whole milk

1½ teaspoons
active dry yeast

3 large eggs plus
1 large egg yolk

3½ cups (17½ oz/545 g)
unbleached flour,
or as needed

1/3 cup (3 oz/90 g) sugar

2 teaspoons orange
blossom honey

1 teaspoon kosher salt

Finely grated zest
of 1 orange

½ cup (4 oz/125 g)
unsalted butter,
cut into tablespoons,
at room temperature

1 large egg beaten with
a pinch of fine sea salt,
for brushing

MAKES 12 ROLLS

1 Make the brioche dough the day before baking. In a small saucepan, warm the milk over medium heat to 110°F (43°C). Pour into a bowl. Sprinkle in the yeast and let stand for 5 minutes. Stir to dissolve the yeast. Add 1 egg and ½ cup (2½ oz/75 g) of the flour and stir well. Sprinkle an additional ½ cup flour over the mixture; do not stir. Cover tightly with plastic wrap. Let stand in a warm place until the starter rises and cracks through the flour topping, about 1 hour.

2 In the bowl of a stand mixer fitted with the paddle attachment, combine the yeast mixture, the remaining 2 eggs and 1 egg yolk, 2 cups (10 oz/315 g) of the flour, the sugar, honey, salt, and orange zest. With the mixer on low speed, add just enough of the remaining flour to make a dough that does not stick to the bowl. Remove the paddle attachment and attach the dough hook. Knead the dough on medium-low speed, adding about ¼ cup (1½ oz/45 g) flour, as needed, until the dough is smooth, 5–7 minutes. Increase the speed to medium and add the butter, one tablespoon at a time, being sure the first addition is absorbed before adding more, to make a soft, sticky dough, about 3 minutes. If the dough sticks to the bowl, add more flour, a little at a time. Shape into a ball.

3 Lightly butter a large bowl and a piece of plastic wrap. Add the dough to the bowl and turn to coat with the butter. Cover the bowl tightly with the plastic wrap, buttered side down. Let the dough rise in a warm spot until it doubles in bulk, about 1½ hours. Punch down the dough, cover again, and refrigerate for at least 8 or up to 24 hours.

4 Butter 12 standard muffin cups. Divide the dough into 12 equal portions. Working with one portion at a time, pinch off a small piece (about one-eighth) and then roll both pieces into balls. Place the larger dough ball in a muffin cup. With a finger, punch a deep hole in the center of the dough, and insert the smaller ball into the hole. Repeat with the remaining dough. Cover with plastic wrap and let stand in a warm place until almost doubled in volume, about 1 hour.

5 Preheat the oven to 350°F (180°C). Remove the plastic wrap and lightly brush the beaten egg over the tops of the brioche. Bake until the brioche are golden brown, 20–25 minutes. Transfer to a wire rack and let cool in the pan for 5 minutes. Remove the rolls from the pan, using the tip of a small knife, if needed. Serve warm.

WALNUT–CHOCOLATE CHIP
BANANA BREAD

3 very ripe bananas, peeled

2 cups (10 oz/315 g) all-purpose flour

1 teaspoon baking soda

¼ teaspoon fine sea salt

6 tablespoons (3 oz/90 g) unsalted butter, at room temperature

¾ cup (6 oz/185 g) sugar

2 large eggs, beaten

½ cup (4 oz/125 g) sour cream, at room temperature

1 cup (6 oz/185 g) semisweet chocolate chips

1 cup (4 oz/125 g) coarsely chopped walnuts, toasted (page 217)

MAKES 1 LOAF

No one can resist a thick slice of freshly baked banana bread, especially when studded with melting chocolate chips and toasty walnuts. Baking this bread is a good way to take advantage of fruit that has been languishing on the counter throughout the busy week. The riper the bananas, the sweeter and more delicious the bread will be.

1 Preheat the oven to 350°F (180°C). Lightly butter a 9-by-5-inch (23-by-13-cm) loaf pan. Line the bottom and long sides of the pan with parchment paper. Butter the top of the parchment. Dust the pan with flour, tapping out the excess.

2 Using a fork, mash the bananas in a bowl; you should have about 1 cup (8 oz/250 g). In another bowl, sift together the flour, baking soda, and salt.

3 In a third bowl, using a handheld mixer on high speed, beat together the butter and sugar until light in color and texture, about 3 minutes. Gradually beat in the eggs and then the mashed bananas. Reduce the speed to low and add the flour mixture in 3 additions alternately with the sour cream in 2 additions, beginning and ending with the flour mixture and stopping to scrape down the bowl as needed, beating until smooth. Fold in the chocolate chips and half of the walnuts. Pour the batter into the prepared pan and smooth the top. Sprinkle the remaining walnuts on top.

4 Bake until a toothpick inserted in the center comes out clean, about 1 hour. Transfer to a wire rack and let cool in the pan for 5 minutes. Turn out onto the rack and remove the paper. Invert again, and let cool completely. Cut into slices and serve warm or at room temperature.

FLAKY CHERRY TURNOVERS

½ recipe (1¼ lb/625 g)
Quick Puff Pastry
(page 215) or 1¼ lb
(625 g) purchased
puff pastry

2½ cups (12½ oz/390 g)
Bing cherries, pitted
and halved

¼ cup (2 oz/60 g)
granulated sugar

1 teaspoon lemon juice

1 tablespoon cornstarch

Flour for rolling out
the dough

1 large egg, beaten

Turbinado sugar
for sprinkling

MAKES 9 TURNOVERS

I find turnovers to be a great excuse to indulge in pie for breakfast. Here, an all-American cherry pie is especially tempting in turnover form, with sweet-tart fruit sealed inside a flaky puff pastry crust—somehow it just tastes better when eaten out of hand. If you still have a craving after cherry season has ended, substitute high-quality canned cherries.

1 Prepare and chill the dough as directed.

2 Have ready a stainless steel bowl set in a larger bowl of ice water. In a heavy, medium saucepan, combine the cherries, sugar, and lemon juice. Cover and cook over medium-low heat, stirring often, until the cherries give off their juices and are tender, about 5 minutes. Taste and add more sugar, if desired. In a small bowl, sprinkle the cornstarch over 1 tablespoon of cold water and stir to dissolve. Stir into the simmering cherry mixture and cook until thickened, about 30 seconds. Transfer to the stainless steel bowl set in the bowl of ice water and let stand until chilled, about 20 minutes.

3 Line a rimmed baking sheet with parchment paper. Roll out the puff pastry on a lightly floured surface into a 15-inch (38-cm) square about ⅛ inch (3 mm) thick. Using a pastry wheel, cut nine 5-inch (13-cm) squares. Place about 2 tablespoons of the chilled filling just off the center of a pastry square. Fold the square in half diagonally so two points meet and enclose the filling. Using a fork, press and seal the edges closed. Place on the baking sheet. Repeat with the remaining pastry squares and filling. Refrigerate, uncovered, for 15–30 minutes.

4 Preheat the oven to 375°F (190°C). Brush the tops of the pastries with some of the beaten egg. Sprinkle the tops with the turbinado sugar. Bake until the turnovers are puffed and golden brown with no sign of uncooked dough, 20–25 minutes. Let cool on the baking sheet for 10–15 minutes. Serve warm or at room temperature.

variation If fresh cherries aren't available, you can substitute one 16-oz (500-g) can good-quality pitted sweet cherries in syrup. Drain the cherries well, reserving ½ cup (4 fl oz/125 ml) of the syrup. In a heavy, small saucepan, combine the drained cherries, the reserved syrup, 1 tablespoon sugar, and the lemon juice. Bring to a simmer over medium heat, stirring often. Stir the dissolved cornstarch into the simmering cherry mixture and cook until thickened, about 30 seconds. Continue as directed in the recipe.

CINNAMON ROLLS
WITH CREAM CHEESE ICING

Sweet Yeast Dough
(page 216)

$\frac{1}{2}$ cup (3$\frac{1}{2}$ oz/105 g)
firmly packed
light brown sugar

6 tablespoons (3 oz/90 g)
unsalted butter,
at room temperature

2 teaspoons
ground cinnamon

Flour for rolling out
the dough

Cream Cheese Icing

1$\frac{1}{2}$ cups (6 oz/185 g)
confectioners' sugar

2 oz (60 g) cream cheese,
at room temperature

2 tablespoons unsalted
butter, at room temperature

$\frac{1}{2}$ teaspoon pure
vanilla extract

Finely grated zest
of 1 orange

$\frac{1}{4}$ cup (2 fl oz/60 ml)
whole milk, or as needed

MAKES 8 ROLLS

The scent of cinnamon rolls baking in the oven is arguably one of life's greatest pleasures. If you like, prepare the dough through Step 4 and refrigerate it overnight, so you can wake up slowly the next morning with a cup of coffee while the rolls bake. I like to make extra-large rolls, and I don't skimp on the thick, orange-scented cream cheese icing.

1 Prepare the dough as directed and let rise for 1$\frac{1}{2}$–2 hours.

2 In a bowl, using a handheld mixer on medium speed, beat together the brown sugar, butter, and cinnamon until combined, about 30 seconds. Set aside.

3 Punch down the dough and turn out onto a floured work surface. Dust the top of the dough with flour. Roll out into a 16-by-14-inch (40-by-35-cm) rectangle, with the long side facing you. Spread the filling evenly over the dough, leaving a 1-inch (2.5-cm) border at the top and bottom. Starting at the long side of the rectangle farthest from you, roll up the rectangle into a log. Pinch the seams to seal. Cut the log crosswise into 8 equal slices with a sharp knife.

4 Butter a 9-by-13-inch (23-by-33-cm) baking pan. Arrange the slices, cut side up, in the pan. Cover loosely with plastic wrap and let rise in a warm spot until doubled in bulk, 75–90 minutes. Or refrigerate overnight until doubled in size, 8–12 hours. Remove from the refrigerator 1 hour before baking.

5 Preheat the oven to 350°F (180°C). Bake until the rolls are golden brown, about 30 minutes. Transfer to a wire rack and let cool in the pan for 15 minutes.

6 Meanwhile, make the icing. Sift the confectioners' sugar into a bowl and add the cream cheese, butter, vanilla, and orange zest. Using a handheld mixer on low speed, beat the mixture until crumbly. Gradually beat in enough of the milk to make a thick but pourable icing. Pour the icing over the warm rolls, and then spread it out evenly using a metal icing spatula. (This makes a thick layer of icing, so use less, if you wish.) Let cool for 15 minutes. Serve warm or at room temperature.

variation Sprinkle $\frac{1}{2}$ cup (3 oz/90 g) raisins, dried cranberries, dried cherries, or chopped toasted pecans (page 217) over the cinnamon butter before rolling up the dough.

STICKY-SWEET
PECAN CARAMEL ROLLS

¼ cup (2 oz/60 g)
vegetable shortening

1¾ cups (14 fl oz/430 ml)
whole milk

⅓ cup (5 oz/155 g) honey

1 package (2¼ teaspoons)
active dry yeast

1 extra-large egg

5–6 cups
(25–30 oz/780–940 g)
all-purpose flour

2 teaspoons kosher salt

2½ cups (20 fl oz/625 ml)
heavy cream

2½ cups (17½ oz/545 g)
plus ⅓ cup (2½ oz/75 g)
firmly packed
dark brown sugar

6 tablespoons (3 oz/90 g)
unsalted butter, melted

⅔ cup (5 oz/155 g)
granulated sugar

1 tablespoon
ground cinnamon

Salted Pecans

2 tablespoons
unsalted butter

1½ cups (6 oz/185 g)
coarsely chopped pecans

1 teaspoon kosher salt

MAKES 12 ROLLS

1 In a saucepan, melt the shortening over low heat. Add the milk and honey and heat to 105°–115°F (40°–46°C). Pour into the bowl of a stand mixer. Sprinkle in the yeast, and let stand for 5 minutes. Stir to dissolve. Stir in the egg. Add 5 cups (25 oz/780 g) of the flour and the salt. Fit the stand mixer with the paddle attachment. With the mixer on low speed, add enough of the remaining flour to make a soft dough that does not stick to the bowl. Remove the paddle attachment and fit the stand mixer with the dough hook attachment. Knead the dough on medium-low speed, adding more flour if needed, until the dough is smooth, 5–7 minutes.

2 Turn out the dough onto a floured work surface. Cut the dough in half, and shape each half into a ball. Place on the floured surface and cover with a moistened kitchen towel. Let the dough rise in a warm spot until it doubles in bulk, about 45 minutes.

3 Meanwhile, in a heavy saucepan, whisk together the cream and 2½ cups (17½ oz/545 g) brown sugar. Bring to a boil over medium heat, whisking frequently. Reduce the heat to medium-low and cook, whisking frequently, until slightly reduced, about 9 minutes. Remove from the heat.

4 Butter a 15-by-10-inch (38-by-25-cm) baking dish with some of the melted butter. Spread 1½ cups (12 fl oz/375 ml) of the caramel sauce into the bottom of the dish. In a bowl, mix together the granulated sugar, ⅓ cup (2½ oz/75 g) brown sugar, and the cinnamon. Roll out 1 ball of dough on a lightly floured work surface into a 15-by-9-inch (38-by-23-cm) rectangle, with the short side facing you. Brush with 1½ tablespoons of the melted butter, leaving a 1-inch (2.5-cm) border at the top. Sprinkle with half of the cinnamon sugar. Starting at the bottom, roll up the dough into a log. Pinch the seam to seal. Cut the log crosswise into 6 slices with a sharp knife. Arrange the slices, cut side up, in the prepared dish. Repeat with the remaining dough, butter, and cinnamon sugar. Cover with the towel and let rise in a warm spot until doubled in bulk, about 45 minutes.

5 To make the salted pecans, in a frying pan, melt the butter over medium heat. Add the pecans and salt and cook, stirring frequently, until toasted, about 3 minutes. Drain on a double thickness of paper towels.

6 Preheat the oven to 350°F (180°C). Bake until the rolls are golden, about 35 minutes. Remove from the oven and brush the rolls with the remaining butter. Let stand for 3 minutes. Place a large rimmed baking sheet over the dish. Using pot holders to protect your hands, hold the baking sheet and dish together, and invert the rolls onto the sheet. Let cool for 5 minutes. Separate the rolls with two forks and let cool for 5–10 minutes more.

7 In a saucepan, warm the remaining sauce over low heat. Serve each roll topped with 3–4 tablespoons of the sauce and a handful of the pecans.

HELL'S KITCHEN MINNEAPOLIS, MN

In the heart of downtown Minneapolis, Hell's Kitchen, whose name gives tribute to the heat and bedlam of a bustling restaurant kitchen, serves three meals a day, seven days a week. Owners Mitch Omer and Steve Meyer eschew fancy cooking to dish up carefully prepared "real food" from scratch. The scene is deliberately irreverent, and the lively, funky atmosphere is a refreshing break from many of the traditional brunch spots (for instance, don't be surprised if your Saturday morning server turns up in curlers and silk pajamas). The extensive menu offers uncommonly fabulous fare, such as wild rice porridge, lemon ricotta pancakes, and four riffs on eggs Benedict. The restaurant's infamous sticky buns come from a family recipe, originally invented by Omer's father. The beloved breakfast pastry reaches new heights here, with a warm, extra-gooey caramel sauce poured on just before serving, then topped with a handful of salted pecans. You'll probably want a fork and a knife to dig into this delicious mess.

BREAD-AND-BUTTER PUDDING
WITH CARAMELIZED PEARS

6 tablespoons (3 oz/90 g)
unsalted butter,
at room temperature

4 ripe pears, such as Anjou
or Comice, peeled, cored,
and cut into eighths

⅓ cup (3 oz/90 g)
plus 2 teaspoons sugar

6 slices day-old challah

2 cups (16 fl oz/500 ml)
whole milk

4 large eggs

1 teaspoon pure
vanilla extract

½ teaspoon
ground cinnamon

Pinch of salt

Confectioners' sugar
for serving

MAKES 4–6 SERVINGS

I think of this indulgent breakfast as a composed version of French toast. It features layers of buttered bread baked into an eggy custard atop a hidden layer of cinnamon-spiced pears. This simple, comforting dish is easy to embellish with other fruits such as apples, peaches, or nectarines.

1 Preheat the oven to 325°F (165°C). Generously grease a 2-quart (2-l) shallow baking dish with 1 tablespoon of the butter.

2 In a large frying pan, melt 2 tablespoons of the butter over medium-high heat. Add the pears and cook, stirring occasionally, until they begin to brown, about 5 minutes. Sprinkle with the 2 teaspoons sugar and stir gently. Cook, stirring occasionally, until the pears begin to caramelize, about 3 minutes more. Spread in the prepared baking dish.

3 Butter one side of each of the bread slices with the remaining 3 tablespoons butter. Cut each bread slice in half. Arrange the bread over the pears, buttered side down, in overlapping rows. In a large bowl, whisk the milk, eggs, ⅓ cup sugar, vanilla, cinnamon, and salt until combined. Pour over the bread. Press the bread lightly to submerge it in the egg mixture. Let stand until the bread has soaked up the egg mixture, 10–15 minutes.

4 Bake until a knife inserted in the center of the bread pudding comes out clean, 30–35 minutes. Remove from the oven and let stand for 5 minutes. Dust lightly with confectioners' sugar. Serve warm.

variation Omit the ground cinnamon and substitute sliced cinnamon-raisin bread (page 124 or purchased) for the challah.

NECTARINE-ALMOND
OVEN PANCAKE

6 tablespoons (3 oz/90 g)
unsalted butter

½ cup (2½ oz/75 g)
all-purpose flour

1 tablespoon
granulated sugar

½ teaspoon fine sea salt

½ cup (4 fl oz/125 ml)
whole milk

3 large eggs, beaten

3 ripe nectarines or
peaches, pitted and sliced
(about 4 cups/24 oz/750 g)

2 tablespoons firmly
packed light brown sugar

2 teaspoons fresh
lemon juice

¼ cup (1 oz/30 g)
sliced almonds, lightly
toasted (page 217)

Confectioners' sugar
for serving

MAKES 4 SERVINGS

Also known as a "Dutch baby," this skillet pancake inflates dramatically in the oven, and falls just as rapidly once removed from the heat. I like to serve it straight from the frying pan, piled with summer nectarines and sliced almonds and dusted with confectioners' sugar.

1 Preheat the oven to 375°F (190°C). Put 4 tablespoons (2 oz/60 g) of the butter in a 10-inch (25-cm) ovenproof frying pan. Heat in the oven until the butter is melted, about 2 minutes. Pour out and reserve 2 tablespoons of the butter; leave the remaining butter in the pan.

2 In a bowl, whisk together the flour, granulated sugar, and salt. Make a well in the center and pour in the milk, eggs, and reserved 2 tablespoons melted butter. Whisk just until combined. Pour into the hot frying pan. Return to the oven and bake until the edges of the pancake are puffed and golden brown, about 20 minutes.

3 Meanwhile, in another frying pan, melt the remaining 2 tablespoons butter over medium heat. Add the nectarines, brown sugar, and lemon juice and cook, stirring occasionally, until the peaches have given off their juices and the brown sugar is melted, about 3 minutes. Remove from the heat.

4 Remove the pan from the oven. Pour the nectarine mixture into the center of the pancake. Sprinkle with the almonds and dust lightly with confectioners' sugar. Cut into wedges and serve hot, directly from the pan.

variation Instead of nectarines or peaches, use any fruit that's in season, such as summer's blueberries and blackberries, or apples and pears in autumn.

SWEET CHEESE PASTRIES
WITH APRICOT GLAZE

Sweet Yeast Dough
(page 216)

5 oz (155 g) cream cheese,
at room temperature

2/3 cup (5 oz/155 g)
ricotta cheese

1 1/3 cups (6 1/2 oz/200 g)
confectioners' sugar

1/2 teaspoon pure
vanilla extract

Finely grated zest
of 1/2 lemon

Flour for rolling out
the dough

1 large egg, beaten

1/3 cup (3 oz/90 g)
apricot preserves

MAKES 12 PASTRIES

The versatile dough can be used for a variety of pastries, such as these cheese-filled sweet rolls, reminiscent of the cheese Danishes from your local bakery.

1 Prepare the dough as directed and let rise for 1 1/2–2 hours.

2 In a bowl, using a handheld mixer on low speed, combine the cream cheese, ricotta, 1/3 cup (2 1/2 oz/75 g) of the sugar, and the vanilla. Stir in the lemon zest. Set aside.

3 Cut the dough in half. On a floured work surface, roll out one of the dough halves into a 15-by-10-inch (38-by-25-cm) rectangle. Cut into six 5-inch (13-cm) squares. Set aside and cover with a kitchen towel. Repeat with the remaining dough.

4 Line two baking sheets with parchment paper. Place a dough square in front of you, with a point at the top. Place a generous tablespoon of the cheese mixture in the center of the square. Take the right corner of dough and stretch it over the cheese mixture; push the corner into the dough to secure it. Pull and stretch the left corner to the right of the cheese to cover it, and press the corner into the dough to secure it. Repeat with the other two corners of dough, stretching the dough over the cheese to completely enclose it. Repeat with the remaining dough and cream cheese mixture. Place the dough packets, spacing them 2 inches (5 cm) apart, on the baking sheets. Loosely cover with plastic wrap and let rise in a warm place until they look puffy, 75–90 minutes.

5 Position a rack in the middle of the oven and another rack in the top third of the oven. Preheat to 350°F (180°C). Brush the tops of the pastries with some of the beaten egg. Place 1 sheet on each oven rack and bake, switching the sheets between the racks and rotating them 180 degrees halfway through baking, until golden brown, 25–30 minutes. Let cool on the baking sheets for 10 minutes.

6 In a small, heavy saucepan, combine the apricot preserves and 1 tablespoon water. Bring to a boil over medium heat, stirring often. Reduce the heat to medium-low and cook until slightly reduced, about 1 minute. Strain through a wire sieve into a small bowl. Sift the remaining 1 cup (4 oz/125 g) sugar into another small bowl. Stir in 1–2 tablespoons water to make a thick, but pourable, glaze. Brush the apricot glaze over the pastries. Drizzle with the sugar glaze. Let stand until the glaze sets, 15–20 minutes. Serve warm or at room temperature.

CINNAMON-RAISIN-SWIRL
BREAKFAST LOAF

½ cup (4 fl oz/125 ml) whole milk

½ cup (4 oz/125 g) sugar

4 tablespoons (2 oz/60 g) unsalted butter, at room temperature, plus 2 tablespoons melted butter for brushing

1 package (2¼ teaspoons) quick-rise yeast

3 cups (15 oz/470 g) bread flour, or as needed

1 teaspoon fine sea salt

2 teaspoons ground cinnamon

½ cup (3 oz/90 g) raisins

MAKES 1 LOAF

The aroma of this classic breakfast bread wafting from the oven will get anyone out of bed in the morning. Try to wait for thirty minutes or so before slicing it, as the cooling period allows the flavors to bloom. After that, cut a slice, slather it with butter, and savor that first amazing bite.

1 In the bowl of a stand mixer fitted with the paddle attachment, combine ½ cup (4 fl oz/125 ml) cold water, the milk, ¼ cup (2 oz/60 g) of the sugar, the 4 tablespoons room temperature butter, and the yeast. Add 2½ cups (12½ oz/390 g) of the flour and the salt. With the mixer on medium-low speed, add enough of the remaining flour to make a soft dough that does not stick to the bowl. Remove the paddle attachment and fit the stand mixer with the dough hook attachment. Knead the dough on medium-low speed, adding more flour if needed, until the dough is smooth but still soft, 6–7 minutes. Shape the dough into a ball.

2 Lightly butter a large bowl. Add the dough and turn to coat with the butter. Cover the bowl tightly with plastic wrap. Let the dough rise in a warm spot until it doubles in bulk, 1¼–1½ hours.

3 Lightly butter a 9-by-5-inch (23-by-13-cm) loaf pan. Punch down the dough and turn out onto a floured work surface. Dust the top of the dough with flour. Roll out into a 9-inch (23-cm) square. In a small bowl, mix together the cinnamon, raisins, and remaining ¼ cup (2 oz/60 g) sugar. Sprinkle evenly over the dough, leaving a ½-inch (12-mm) border around all sides. Roll up the dough into a log and pinch the seam to seal. Transfer to the loaf pan, seam side down, and lightly press the top of the dough to evenly fill the pan. Loosely cover with plastic wrap. Let stand in a warm spot until the dough rises to the top of the pan, about 1 hour.

4 Preheat the oven to 350°F (180°C). Brush the loaf gently with the melted butter. Bake until the top of the loaf is golden brown and the bottom, when the loaf is carefully removed from the pan, sounds hollow when rapped on the bottom with your knuckles, 35–40 minutes. Transfer to a wire rack and let cool in the pan for 10 minutes. Invert onto the rack, then invert again and let cool for at least 30 minutes before slicing.

SWEET ALMOND BUNS
WITH CARDAMOM

¾ cup (6 fl oz/180 ml)
whole milk

¼ cup (2 oz/60 g) plus
2 tablespoons sugar

4 tablespoons (2 oz/60 g)
unsalted butter,
at room temperature

1 large egg

1 package (2¼ teaspoons)
quick-rise yeast

¼ teaspoon freshly
ground cardamom

¼ teaspoon almond extract

1¾ cups (9 oz/280 g)
unbleached flour

½ teaspoon fine sea salt

½ cup (2½ oz/75 g) finely
chopped almonds

MAKES 12 BUNS

Traditional Scandinavian sweet breads usually feature either almonds or raisins, and tend to include cardamom, a richly scented spice that has inspired a dedicated following among lovers of baked goods. Cardamom loses its flavor quickly after grinding, so I buy whole cardamom pods, remove the seeds, and grind them with a coffee grinder.

◇◇

1 In the bowl of a stand mixer fitted with the paddle attachment, combine the milk, ¼ cup sugar, the butter, egg, yeast, cardamom, and almond extract. Add the flour and salt. Mix on low speed until a thick batter forms, about 2 minutes. Add ⅓ cup (1½ oz/45 g) of the almonds and mix just until combined.

2 Butter and flour 12 standard muffin cups. (The batter is too sticky to use paper liners.) Divide the batter evenly among the muffin cups. Lightly oil a sheet of plastic wrap and place it over the pan, oiled side down. Let stand in a warm spot until the buns have risen to the top of the pan, about 1 hour.

3 Preheat the oven to 350°F (180°C). In a small bowl, combine the remaining almonds and the 2 tablespoons sugar. Sprinkle evenly over the tops of the buns. Bake until the buns are golden brown, 20–25 minutes.

4 Transfer to a wire rack and let cool in the pan for 10 minutes. Remove the buns from the pan and serve warm.

OLD-FASHIONED
GLAZED CHOCOLATE DOUGHNUTS

2¼ cups (11½ oz/360 g)
plus 2 tablespoons
all-purpose flour

½ cup (1½ oz/45 g)
plus 2 tablespoons
Dutch-process
cocoa powder

1¾ teaspoons
baking powder

¼ teaspoon fine sea salt

1 cup (8 oz/250 g) sugar

2 large eggs,
at room temperature

½ cup (4 fl oz/125 ml)
whole milk

4 tablespoons (2 oz/60 g)
unsalted butter,
melted and cooled

1 teaspoon
pure vanilla extract

Canola oil for deep-frying

Chocolate Icing (page 216)

Multicolored sprinkles
for decorating (optional)

MAKES 12 DOUGHNUTS

1 To make the doughnuts, in a bowl, sift together the 2¼ cups flour, the ½ cup cocoa powder, the baking powder, and salt. In another bowl, using a handheld mixer on high speed, beat the sugar and eggs until thickened and very light in color, about 3 minutes. In a third bowl, whisk together the milk, melted butter, and vanilla. Pour the milk mixture over the flour mixture and stir just until moistened. Add the egg mixture and stir until combined. The dough will be very sticky.

2 Line a rimmed baking sheet with parchment paper. Transfer the dough to the baking sheet, cover with another sheet of parchment paper, and roll out the dough until about ¾ inch (2 cm) thick. Refrigerate until firm, at least 2 or up to 4 hours.

3 Pour oil to a depth of at least 3 inches (7.5 cm) into a heavy, deep saucepan and heat over high heat to 340°F (170°C) on a deep-frying thermometer. Set a large wire rack on another rimmed baking sheet and place near the stove. In a small bowl, sift together the remaining 2 tablespoons each of flour and cocoa. Dust the work surface with some of the cocoa mixture. Remove the dough from the refrigerator. Remove the top parchment paper, invert the chilled dough onto the work surface, and remove the remaining paper. Line the baking sheet with a fresh sheet of parchment paper. Dust the top of the dough with some of the cocoa mixture. Using a rolling pin, roll out the dough until ½ inch (12 mm) thick. Using a 3-inch (7.5-cm) doughnut cutter and dipping the cutter into the cocoa mixture before each cut, cut out as many doughnuts as possible, pressing straight down and lifting straight up. Transfer the doughnuts to the parchment-lined baking sheet. Gather up the scraps (including the holes) and continue rolling and cutting to make 12 doughnuts.

4 Using a metal spatula, carefully lower a few of the doughnuts into the hot oil, being sure not to crowd the pan. Deep-fry the doughnuts, turning them once at the halfway point, until the surfaces look set, about 3 minutes. Using a wire skimmer, transfer to the rack to drain. Repeat until all of the doughnuts have been fried. Let cool.

5 Pour the icing into a bowl wide enough to fit a doughnut. Holding each doughnut by its edges, briefly dip it, smooth side down, into the icing, letting the excess drip back into the bowl. Place on the wire rack, iced side up. You will have leftover icing, so dip the doughnuts again, if you wish. Scatter the sprinkles, if using, on top of each doughnut. Let stand until the icing is set, about 30 minutes. Serve at room temperature.

HOTCHOCOLATE CHICAGO, IL

Mindy's HotChocolate Restaurant and Dessert Bar has a name that may belie its truly fabulous lunch and dinner offerings, but hot drinks and chef Mindy Segal's award winning pastries are really the restaurant's claim to fame. On Saturday and Sunday mornings, lines quickly form on North Damen Avenue, with diners hungry for the opportunity to dip into both the sweet and savory sides of the menu. Most of them are easily tempted to start off their brunch with a basket of the freshly baked breakfast breads, which include the delectable pull-apart orange blossom monkey bread with strawberry caramel sauce. Whether a fresh scramble or a platter of smoked fish ensue, they are sure to be accompanied by one of the namesake drinks: six different versions of hot chocolate, from light to dark, espresso-infused to cinnamon-spiced, all served with house-made marshmallows. This streamlined version of Segal's monkey bread takes a few shortcuts to the original, but it is equally delicious.

MONKEY BREAD
WITH STRAWBERRY CARAMEL SAUCE

Orange Brioche dough
(page 109)

1 pint (8 oz/250 g)
strawberries, hulled and
cut in half lengthwise

1 cup (8 oz/250 g) plus
2 tablespoons sugar

½ cup (4 fl oz/125 ml)
heavy cream

½ cup (4 fl oz/125 ml)
fresh orange juice

2 tablespoons
light corn syrup

1 teaspoon
orange blossom water

½ teaspoon
fresh lemon juice

Finely grated
zest of 1 orange

Kosher salt

Melted butter for brushing

Flour for rolling out
the dough

⅓ cup (1½ oz/45 g)
sliced almonds, toasted
(page 217)

MAKES 8 SERVINGS

1 Prepare the brioche dough as directed through Step 3.

2 In a bowl, combine the strawberries and the 2 tablespoons sugar. Cover and let stand at room temperature, stirring occasionally, until the berries give off at least 2 tablespoons of juice, at least 2 hours or up to overnight. In a small saucepan, cook the strawberries and their juices over medium heat, stirring occasionally, until the strawberries are soft and the juices are syrupy, about 3 minutes. Drain in a coarse-mesh sieve, reserving the strawberries and their juices separately.

3 In a small saucepan, combine the cream and orange juice and heat over medium heat until warmed; set aside. In a heavy, medium saucepan, combine the 1 cup sugar and the corn syrup. Bring to a boil over medium-high heat, stirring constantly, until the sugar melts. Continue cooking, without stirring, as the mixture caramelizes. Wash down any sugar crystals that form inside the pan with a pastry brush dipped in cold water and occasionally swirl the pot by its handle, until the mixture turns dark amber, about 5 minutes. A few tablespoons at a time, carefully stir in the warm cream mixture (it will bubble up), returning to a boil after each addition, then boil for 1 minute more. Remove from the heat and stir in the orange blossom water, lemon juice, orange zest, and reserved strawberry juices. Season with a pinch of salt. Let the sauce cool completely.

4 Generously brush eight 1-cup (8–fl oz/250-ml) ramekins or cocottes with the melted butter. Turn out the dough onto a floured surface. Divide into 8 equal portions. Cut each portion into 6 equal pieces and roll into balls to make 48 balls total.

5 In a bowl, combine the drained reserved strawberries with ⅓ cup (3 fl oz/80 ml) of the cooled caramel sauce. Divide the mixture evenly among the prepared ramekins. Pour ½ cup (4 fl oz/125 ml) of the remaining caramel sauce into the same bowl. For each serving, add 6 balls to the sauce, turn with a rubber spatula to coat well, and transfer to a ramekin, fitting the balls as evenly as possible. Repeat with the remaining balls and ramekins, adding more caramel sauce, if needed. Reserve the remaining caramel sauce. Place the ramekins on a rimmed baking sheet. Lightly oil a sheet of plastic wrap and place it over the ramekins, oiled side down. Let the dough rise in a warm spot until it doubles in bulk, about 1¼ hours.

6 Preheat the oven to 350°F (180°C). Remove the plastic wrap from the ramekins and bake the monkey bread until golden brown, about 30 minutes.

7 In a small saucepan, warm the reserved caramel sauce over medium heat. Brush the tops of each monkey bread with some of the reserved caramel sauce, sprinkle with the toasted almonds, and serve.

NEW ORLEANS–STYLE
BEIGNETS

½ cup (4 fl oz/125 ml)
heavy cream

¼ cup (2 oz/60 g)
granulated sugar

2 tablespoons unsalted
butter, at room temperature

1 large egg, beaten

1 package (2¼ teaspoons)
quick-rise yeast

3¾ cups (19 oz/590 g)
all-purpose flour,
or as needed

½ teaspoon fine sea salt

Canola oil for deep-frying

Confectioners' sugar
for serving

**MAKES ABOUT
40 BEIGNETS**

Beignet means "fried dough" in French, and refers to one of the great contributions of Louisiana Creole cuisine to Southern culinary tradition. The recipe makes a sizeable amount, but no one can eat just one of these bite-sized treats. My suggestion: invite some friends over, and dig in!

1 In the bowl of a stand mixer fitted with the paddle attachment, combine ¾ cup (6 fl oz/180 ml) cold water, the cream, sugar, butter, egg, and yeast. Add 3 cups (15 oz/470 g) of the flour and the salt. With the mixer on medium-low speed, add enough of the remaining flour to make a soft dough that does not stick to the bowl. Remove the paddle attachment and fit the stand mixer with the dough hook attachment. Knead the dough on medium-low speed, adding more flour if needed, until the dough is smooth but still soft, 6–7 minutes. Shape into a ball.

2 Lightly butter a large bowl. Add the dough and turn to coat with the butter. Cover the bowl tightly with plastic wrap. Let the dough rise in a warm spot until it doubles in bulk, 1½–2 hours. Or, refrigerate overnight until doubled in size, 8–12 hours; remove from the refrigerator 1 hour before proceeding.

3 Line 2 baking sheets with parchment paper. Punch down the dough and turn out onto a floured work surface. Dust the top of the dough with flour. Roll out into a large rectangle about ¼ inch (6 mm) thick. Using a pizza wheel or a sharp knife, diagonally cut the dough into 2-inch (5-cm) strips. Cut in the other direction, also in diagonal 2-inch (5-cm) strips, to create diamond shapes. Transfer to the baking sheets and loosely cover with plastic wrap. Let stand in a warm spot until the beignets rise slightly, about 15 minutes.

4 Preheat the oven to 200°F (95°C). Place a wire rack over a rimmed baking sheet. Pour the oil to a depth of at least 3 inches (7.5 cm) into a deep, heavy saucepan and heat to 350°F (180°C) on a deep-frying thermometer.

5 Using a metal spatula, carefully lower a few of the beignets into the hot oil, being sure not to crowd the pan. Deep-fry the beignets, turning often, until puffed and golden brown, about 3 minutes. Using a wire skimmer, transfer to the rack to drain. Keep warm in the oven. Repeat until all of the beignets have been fried. Arrange the beignets on a serving plate, generously dust with confectioners' sugar, and serve at once.

LEMON-GLAZED
RASPBERRY JAM DOUGHNUTS

1 cup (8 fl oz/250 ml) whole milk

3 large eggs

4 tablespoons (2 oz/60 g) unsalted butter, melted and cooled

¼ cup (2 oz/60 g) sugar

1 package (2¼ teaspoons) quick-rise yeast

4¼ cups (21½ oz/675 g) all-purpose flour, or as needed

½ teaspoon fine sea salt

Canola oil for deep-frying

1¼ cups (12½ oz/390 g) raspberry preserves

Lemon Icing (page 216)

MAKES ABOUT 16 DOUGHNUTS

1 In the bowl of a stand mixer fitted with the paddle attachment, combine the milk, eggs, butter, sugar, and yeast. Add 3½ cups (17½ oz/545 g) of the flour and the salt. With the mixer on low speed, add enough of the remaining flour to make a soft dough that does not stick to the bowl. Replace the paddle attachment with the dough hook attachment. Knead the dough on medium-low speed, adding more flour if needed, until the dough is smooth but still soft and sticky, about 6 minutes.

2 Lightly butter a large bowl. Add the dough and turn to coat with the butter. Cover the bowl tightly with plastic wrap. Let the dough rise in a warm spot until it doubles in bulk, 1½–2 hours. Or refrigerate overnight until doubled in size, at least 8 or up to 12 hours, and remove from the refrigerator 1 hour before proceeding.

3 Line a large baking sheet with parchment paper. Punch down the dough and turn out onto a floured work surface. Dust the top of the dough with flour. Roll out the dough into a 12-inch (30-cm) square about ½ inch (12 mm) thick. Using a 3-inch (7.5-cm) round biscuit cutter, cut out as many rounds of dough as possible. Transfer the rounds to the baking sheet. Gather up the scraps and continue rolling and cutting to make about 16 doughnuts. Loosely cover the doughnuts with plastic wrap and let stand in a warm spot until slightly puffed, 15–20 minutes.

4 Pour oil to a depth of at least 3 inches (7.5 cm) into a heavy, deep saucepan and heat over high heat to 340°F (170°C) on a deep-frying thermometer. Set a large wire rack on another rimmed baking sheet and place near the stove. Using a metal spatula, carefully lower a few of the doughnuts into the hot oil, being sure not to crowd the pan. Deep-fry the doughnuts, turning them once at the halfway point, until golden brown, about 3 minutes. If any bubbles form under the surface of the dough during frying, pierce them with the tip of a sharp knife. Using a wire skimmer, transfer the doughnuts to the rack to drain. Repeat to fry the remaining doughnuts. Let cool.

5 Transfer the preserves to a pastry bag fitted with a ¼-inch (6-mm) plain tip. Using a small, sharp knife, cut a slit into the side and extending into the center of a doughnut. Insert the pastry tip into the slit until it reaches the center of the doughnut and pipe in a generous tablespoonful of preserves. Repeat with the remaining doughnuts and preserves.

6 Place the lemon glaze in a small bowl at least 4 inches (10 cm) wide. Holding each doughnut by its edges, briefly dip it into the glaze, letting the excess glaze drip back into the bowl. Place on the wire rack, iced side up. You will have leftover glaze, so dip the doughnuts again, if you wish. Let stand until the icing is set, about 30 minutes. Serve at room temperature (preferably the same day they are made).

APPLE FRITTERS
WITH CIDER GLAZE

1³/₄ cups (9 oz/280 g)
all-purpose flour

¹/₃ cup (3 oz/90 g)
granulated sugar

2 teaspoons baking powder

¹/₂ teaspoon
ground cinnamon

¹/₄ teaspoon freshly
ground nutmeg

¹/₂ teaspoon fine sea salt

¹/₂ cup (4 fl oz/125 ml)
whole milk

1 large egg

2 tablespoons unsalted
butter, melted and cooled

1 cup (4 oz/125 g) peeled,
cored, and diced apples
such as Golden Delicious
or Empire

Canola oil for deep-frying

1 cup (4 oz/125 g)
confectioners' sugar

2 tablespoons apple cider,
or as needed

MAKES 6 FRITTERS

I remember with fondness the lumpy, slightly misshapen apple fritters that appeared in the display cases of doughnut shops up and down the west coast of California, where I grew up. While some commercial examples mimic the size of hubcaps, this recipe makes much more manageable fritters, perfect for frying up a fresh batch at home.

1 In a bowl, sift together the flour, granulated sugar, baking powder, cinnamon, nutmeg, and salt. In another bowl, whisk together the milk, egg, and butter. Pour the milk mixture over the flour mixture and stir just until moistened. Stir in the apples.

2 Line a large baking sheet with parchment paper, and dust the parchment paper with flour. Transfer the dough to the baking sheet. The dough will be very sticky. Using floured hands, pat out into a rectangle ¹/₂ inch (12 mm) thick. Refrigerate for 15 minutes to chill and slightly firm the dough.

3 Place a wire rack over a rimmed baking sheet. Pour oil to a depth of 3 inches (7.5 cm) into a heavy, deep saucepan and heat the oil over high heat to 350°F (180°C) on a deep-frying thermometer.

4 Using a 3-inch (7.5-cm) biscuit cutter, cut out as many rounds of the dough as possible. Gather up the scraps, knead briefly, and continue patting and cutting out to make 6 rounds. Using your hands, shape each round into an oval, maintaining the ¹/₂ inch (12 mm) thickness.

5 Using a metal spatula, carefully lower 3 ovals into the hot oil, being sure not to crowd the pan. Deep-fry the fritters, turning once at the halfway point, until golden brown, about 3 minutes. Using a wire skimmer, transfer to the rack to drain. Repeat until all of the fritters have been fried. Let cool.

6 To make the glaze, sift the confectioners' sugar into a wide bowl at least 4 inches (10 cm) wide. Whisk in enough cider to make a glaze that is slightly thicker than heavy cream. Holding each fritter by its edges, briefly dip it into the glaze, letting the excess drip back into the bowl. Place on the wire rack, iced side up. You will have leftover icing, so dip the fritters again, if you wish. Let stand until the icing is set, about 30 minutes. Serve at room temperature (preferably the same day they are made).

MAPLE-COCONUT GRANOLA

WITH YOGURT AND MANGO

3 cups (9 oz/280 g) rolled oats

2 cups (10 oz/315 g) coarsely chopped almonds, pecans, or walnuts

1 cup (4 oz/125 g) shredded dried coconut flakes

1 cup (4 oz/125 g) hulled, unsalted raw sunflower seeds

1/2 cup (3 1/2 oz/105 g) firmly packed light brown sugar

1/2 cup (5 1/2 oz/170 g) pure maple syrup, preferably Grade B

1/3 cup (3 fl oz/80 ml) vegetable oil

1 teaspoon ground cinnamon

1 1/2 cups (9 oz/280 g) raisins

For each serving

1/2 cup (2 1/2 oz/75 g) Maple-Coconut Granola

1/2 cup (4 oz/125 g) plain Greek yogurt

1/2 cup (3 oz/90 g) peeled, pitted, and diced ripe mango

Honey for drizzling

**MAKES 10 CUPS
(3 LB/1.5 KG)**

I love making my own granola, because it allows for so much variation. Use any dried fruit you like, such as chopped apricots, cherries, figs, or dates, in place of the raisins. You can also choose your favorite type of nuts. Serve this the traditional way in a bowl with milk, or layer it with thick Greek yogurt and sweet mango cubes or fresh berries.

1 Preheat the oven to 300°F (150°C). Lightly oil a deep roasting pan.

2 Add the oats, almonds, coconut, and sunflower seeds to the prepared pan. Mix well. In a bowl, whisk together the brown sugar, maple syrup, oil, and cinnamon until the sugar dissolves. Pour over the oat mixture and mix well with your hands until the mixture is thoroughly moistened.

3 Bake, stirring every 10 minutes and being sure to move the granola from the edges of the pan into the center, until it is noticeably crisper, 45–55 minutes. Remove from the oven and let cool completely in the pan. Stir in the raisins. (The granola can be stored at room temperature in an airtight container for up to 1 month.)

4 For each serving, combine the granola, yogurt, and mango cubes in a bowl. (Or layer the ingredients in a large parfait glass.) Drizzle with honey and serve at once.

STEEL-CUT OATS
WITH HONEYED PEARS AND GLAZED PECANS

¼ teaspoon fine sea salt

1 cup (6 oz/185 g)
steel-cut oats

1 tablespoon plus
1 teaspoon unsalted butter

½ cup (2 oz/60 g) pecans

2 teaspoons sugar

2 ripe, juicy pears, such as
Comice or Anjou, peeled,
cored, and cut into chunks

3 tablespoons honey

¼ teaspoon
ground cinnamon

Half-and-half, cream,
or milk for serving

MAKES 4 SERVINGS

Steel-cut oats result in a textured oatmeal, with a deliciously chewy yet tender bite. They do require longer simmering than regular oatmeal, but to me it's worth it. If you're short on time, soak the oats overnight to reduce the cooking time to 5–10 minutes. Top with crunchy sugared pecans and cinnamon-coated pears, and you'll be in oatmeal heaven.

1 In a medium, heavy-bottomed saucepan, bring 4 cups (32 fl oz/1 l) water and the salt to a boil over high heat. Stir in the oats and return to a boil. Reduce the heat to medium-low. Simmer, uncovered, stirring often to avoid scorching, until the oats are done to your preferred texture, 25–35 minutes.

2 In a frying pan, melt the 1 teaspoon butter over medium heat. Add the pecans and sprinkle with the sugar. Cook, stirring constantly, until the sugar melts and the pecans are toasted and glazed, about 1 minute. Transfer to a chopping board. Let the pecans cool slightly, then coarsely chop. Set aside. Rinse out the frying pan.

3 Just before the oatmeal is done, melt the 1 tablespoon butter over medium heat in the same frying pan. Add the pears and cook, stirring occasionally, until they have given off some juices and they are heated through, about 3 minutes. Add the honey and cinnamon and stir just until the honey melts.

4 Divide the oatmeal among 4 bowls. Top with equal amounts of the pears and their juices, and the pecans. Drizzle each serving with some half-and-half and serve hot.

variation Substitute Golden Delicious apples for the pears. To spice things up, add a sprinkling of minced crystallized ginger to the topping.

4 SAVORY DELIGHTS

GRILLED CHEDDAR SANDWICHES
WITH BACON AND TOMATO

4–6 thick slices applewood-smoked bacon

4 slices country-style bread

¼ lb (125 g) sharp farmhouse Cheddar cheese, thinly sliced

4 thick slices ripe tomato, drained on paper towels

2 tablespoons unsalted butter, at room temperature

MAKES 2 SANDWICHES

A grilled cheese sandwich, with its crunchy, toasted exterior and melting center, is high on my list of comfort foods. Since it's comprised of just a few simple ingredients, quality will make all the difference, so seek out a true farmhouse Cheddar, some seriously thick applewood-smoked bacon, and the juiciest, most flavorful tomatoes you can find.

1 In a large frying pan, fry the bacon over medium heat until crisp and brown, about 8 minutes. Transfer to paper towels to drain. Discard the fat in the pan. Cut each bacon slice in half crosswise.

2 Lay two of the bread slices on a work surface and top each with one-fourth of the cheese, 2 slices of tomato, half of the bacon, and the remaining cheese. Top with the remaining two bread slices. Spread the outsides of each sandwich with 1 tablespoon of the butter.

3 Return the frying pan to medium heat. Add the sandwiches. Place a flat lid or a heatproof plate on the sandwiches to weight them down. Cook until the undersides are golden brown and the cheese starts to melt, about 2 minutes. Flip the sandwiches, weight them down with the lid, and brown the other sides, about 2 minutes more. Cut each sandwich in half and serve at once.

TOMATO TART
WITH BASIL AND RICOTTA

½ recipe (1¼ lb/625 g) Quick Puff Pastry (page 215) or 1¼ lb (625 g) purchased puff pastry

Flour for rolling out the dough

1¼ cups (10 oz/315 g) ricotta cheese

½ cup (2 oz/60 g) freshly grated Parmesan cheese

2 large eggs

3 tablespoons minced fresh basil, plus chopped basil for garnish

Kosher salt and freshly ground pepper

⅛ teaspoon freshly grated nutmeg

4 large tomatoes, preferably heirloom

1 tablespoon olive oil

MAKES 8 SERVINGS

Here, flaky puff pastry replaces pizza dough for a light, Italian-inspired tart. Forming the tart by hand, instead of confining it to a tart pan, gives it a rustic look well suited to the colorful combination of creamy white ricotta, fragrant green basil, and tangy heirloom tomatoes. Seeding the tomatoes prevents the bottom of the tart from getting soggy.

1 Prepare and chill the dough as directed.

2 Preheat the oven to 375°F (190°C). Cut a piece of parchment paper to fit a 16-by-11-inch (40-cm-by-28-cm) rimmed baking sheet. Turn the baking sheet over, and place the parchment on the underside. Roll out the puff pastry on a floured work surface into a 16-by-11-inch (40-cm-by-28-cm) rectangle about ⅛ inch (3 mm) thick. Transfer the dough to the parchment paper. Refrigerate the dough on the baking sheet for 15 minutes.

3 In a bowl, mix the ricotta, Parmesan, 1 of the eggs, the 3 tablespoons minced basil, ¼ teaspoon salt, ¼ teaspoon pepper, and the nutmeg. Set aside.

4 Using a serrated knife, slice the tomatoes into rounds about ½-inch (12-mm) thick. Shake out the majority of the seeds (don't worry if a few seeds remain). Place on paper towels to drain briefly. Season the tomatoes with salt and pepper.

5 Remove the pastry from the refrigerator. Using a pizza wheel, trim the rough edges from the pastry. Using the tip of a small sharp knife, score a 1-inch (2.5-cm) border inside the edges of the pastry, taking care not to cut through the pastry. Score the border with diagonal marks about 1 inch (2.5 cm) apart. Pierce the pastry inside the border with a fork. Spread the ricotta mixture evenly inside the border, then top with the tomato slices. Drizzle the olive oil over the tomatoes and filling. In a small bowl, beat the remaining egg. Lightly brush the pastry border with some of the egg.

6 Bake until the crust is golden brown, 25–30 minutes. Let cool for 3–5 minutes. Cut the pastry into 8 equal pieces. Transfer to a serving platter, sprinkle with chopped basil, and serve warm.

variation You can use just about any seasonal tomatoes, such as plum or cherry, adjusting the amount as needed to cover the ricotta filling.

BREAKFAST FLATBREAD
WITH PROSCIUTTO AND TOMATO

Flatbread Dough

1 tablespoon (½ oz) packed fresh yeast or 1¾ teaspoons quick-rise yeast

1½ teaspoons sugar

2 cups (10 oz/315 g) bread flour

1½ teaspoons fine sea salt

2 teaspoons olive oil

1 cup (5 oz/155 g) unbleached all-purpose flour, or as needed

Flatbread toppings

¼ cup (2 fl oz/60 ml) olive oil

2 cloves garlic, crushed

1½ cups (6 oz/185 g) shredded fresh mozzarella cheese

2 ripe heirloom tomatoes, thinly sliced, drained on paper towels

¾ cup (6 oz/185 g) ricotta cheese

12 thin slices prosciutto

6 Fried Eggs (page 211)

Freshly ground pepper

MAKES 6 SERVINGS

1 To make the flatbread dough, in the bowl of a stand mixer, combine 1 cup (8 fl oz/250 ml) warm water (105°–115°F/40°–46°C) and the yeast (or 1 cup cold water and the quick-rise yeast). Let stand for 5 minutes, then stir to dissolve. Add the sugar, bread flour, and salt. Fit the stand mixer with the paddle attachment and mix on low speed until a batter forms. Add the 2 teaspoons oil. Gradually add enough of the all-purpose flour to make a soft dough that does not stick to the bowl. Remove the paddle attachment and attach the dough hook. Knead the dough on medium-low speed, adding more flour if needed, until smooth, 5–7 minutes.

2 Lightly oil a large rimmed baking sheet. Turn the dough out onto a floured work surface. Divide the dough into 6 equal portions and form each into a taut ball. Place on the baking sheet, smooth side up, and loosely cover with plastic wrap. Let stand in a warm spot until the dough doubles in bulk, about 1 hour. (The dough can be refrigerated for up to 1 day; remove 1 hour before using.)

3 Prepare an outdoor grill for medium-high heat. Line another baking sheet with parchment paper. Oil the parchment paper, then dust with flour. Lightly oil both sides of an additional 6 sheets of parchment paper. On a lightly floured work surface, shape 1 ball of dough into a flat disk. Using a rolling pin, roll out the dough into a very thin round about 10 inches (25 cm) in diameter. Transfer to the baking sheet, dust with flour, and top with a sheet of oiled parchment. Repeat with the remaining dough.

4 Have ready a rimmed baking sheet. Brush and oil the grill grates. In batches, slide the dough rounds onto the grill. Grill until brown grill marks appear on the undersides of the rounds, 15–30 seconds. Flip the dough and grill the other sides until marked. Transfer to the baking sheet.

5 Place a baking stone in the oven and preheat to 500°F (260°C). In a small saucepan, heat the ¼ cup oil and the garlic just until small bubbles form around the garlic. Strain the oil into a bowl and let cool. Discard the garlic.

6 Brush each flatbread with some of the garlic oil. Place on a pizza peel or rimless baking sheet. Sprinkle with ¼ cup (1 oz/30 g) mozzarella cheese and top with a few tomato slices. Dot with about 2 tablespoons ricotta. Slide the flatbread onto the baking stone and bake until the mozzarella is melted and bubbling, about 4 minutes. Depending on the size of the baking stone, you should be able to bake 2 flatbreads at a time. Transfer each flatbread to a plate. Drape 2 prosciutto slices over each flatbread, and top with a fried egg. Using a pizza wheel, cut into wedges. Grind pepper over each flatbread, drizzle with garlic oil, and serve at once.

variation Instead of grilling the dough rounds, you can prebake them, one at a time, on a baking stone in a preheated 500°F (260°C) oven until set and very lightly browned, about 4 minutes.

UNIVERSAL CAFE SAN FRANCISCO, CA

Growing up, Leslie Carr Avalos spent her summers tending the family vegetable patch in upstate New York, giving her a life-long appreciation of organic produce. Now as chef and owner of Universal Cafe, Carr Avalos shows off her philosophy with an ever-changing menu that reflects the best of the season. Tucked among the Victorians on a residential block of the sunny Potrero Hill neighborhood of San Francisco, the legendary brunch inspires long waits, although hungry patrons are placated with a fresh ginger lemonade or strawberry bellini from the bar. The food doesn't disappoint, as Carr Avalos loves to reinvent familiar brunch dishes—omelets, French toast, and various egg incarnations serve as springboards showcasing local produce, meats, seafood, and dairy products. A prime example is a deliciously simple flatbread, which features Italian charcuterie, California tomatoes, and a farm fresh egg cracked right on top. Feel free to create your own toppings based on what's fresh at your farmers' market.

OPEN-FACED GOAT CHEESE AND
ROASTED MUSHROOM SANDWICHES

8 portobello mushrooms

6 tablespoons
(3 fl oz/90 ml) olive oil

Kosher salt and freshly
ground pepper

1 tablespoon plus
1 teaspoon
balsamic vinegar

4 large, wide slices
crusty rustic bread,
such as levain

1 clove garlic, halved

4 oz (125 g) rindless
goat cheese (chèvre),
at room temperature

4 oz (125 g) baby spinach

MAKES 4 SERVINGS

To push these sandwiches over the top, I roast the mushrooms—the dry heat of the oven concentrates their juices and enhances their meaty texture. Heap them on slices of toasted country-style bread, top with goat cheese and a handful of spinach, and you have a hearty, fork-and-knife vegetarian breakfast that even carnivores will love.

1 Position one rack in the middle of the oven and a second rack in the top third of the oven. Preheat the oven to 425°F (220°C). Lightly oil a rimmed baking sheet. Cut the stems from the mushrooms where they meet the caps. Brush the stems and caps with 2 tablespoons of the olive oil. Place on the prepared baking sheet and season with salt and pepper. Roast on the middle rack until the mushrooms are tender and juicy, about 15 minutes. Transfer to a carving board. Cut the stems in half lengthwise. Cover loosely with foil to keep warm.

2 Meanwhile, in a small bowl, whisk together the balsamic vinegar, ⅛ teaspoon salt, and a couple grinds of pepper. Gradually whisk in the remaining 4 tablespoons (2 fl oz/60 ml) olive oil. Set aside.

3 A few minutes before the mushrooms are done, place the bread slices directly on the upper oven rack, and bake until lightly toasted, about 5 minutes. Rub one side of each bread slice with the cut sides of the garlic, then spread each slice with 1 oz (30 g) of the goat cheese.

4 For each serving, place a bread slice, cheese side up, on a serving plate. Top with 2 portobello mushroom caps and stems. Add a handful of spinach, dividing it evenly among the sandwiches. Drizzle with the vinaigrette and serve at once.

GRILLED PANINI

WITH PROSCIUTTO AND MOZZARELLA

8 slices firm white
country bread

6 tablespoons (3 fl oz/
90 ml) pesto, homemade
(page 213) or purchased

½ lb (250 g) fresh
whole-milk mozzarella,
thinly sliced

½ lb (250 g) prosciutto,
thinly sliced

¼ cup (2 oz/60 g)
unsalted butter,
at room temperature

MAKES 4 PANINI

Italian-style panini (which are essentially embellished grilled cheese sandwiches) are starting to show up on menus across the country—and for good reason. I love to make these sandwiches as a late-morning meal, verging on lunch. For the best results, choose a good-quality, firm bread that doesn't have too many holes.

1 Lay the bread slices on a work surface and spread each slice with the pesto, dividing it evenly. Divide the cheese and prosciutto evenly among 4 of the bread slices. Top with the remaining bread slices. Spread each sandwich on both sides with 1 tablespoon of the butter.

2 Preheat the oven to 200°F (95°C). Heat a grill pan or heavy frying pan over medium-high heat, or heat a panini press. Add 2 sandwiches. Place another heavy pan on the sandwiches to weight them down. Cook, adjusting the heat as needed so the panini do not brown too quickly, until the undersides are lightly browned, 2–3 minutes. Flip the sandwiches, weight them with the pan, and brown the other sides until the cheese melts, about 2 minutes more. If using a panini press, the total cooking time will be 4–5 minutes. Remove from the pan and transfer to a baking sheet; keep warm in the oven while cooking the remaining sandwiches in the same way.

3 Cut each sandwich in half diagonally and serve at once.

variation If you aren't in the mood for prosciutto, other Italian-style cured meats, such as salami and mortadella, also make wonderful panini.

FONTINA, LEEK, AND
MUSHROOM BRAID

½ recipe (1¼ lb/625 g)
Quick Puff Pastry (page 215)
or 1¼ lb (625 g)
purchased puff pastry

2 tablespoons
unsalted butter

3 leeks, white and pale
green parts only, chopped
(about 2 cups/8 oz/250 g)

12 oz (375 g) cremini or
white mushrooms, sliced

½ cup (4 fl oz/125 ml)
heavy cream

1 teaspoon minced thyme

½ cup (2 oz/60 g)
shredded fontina cheese

Kosher salt and
freshly ground pepper

Flour for rolling out
the dough

1 large egg, beaten

MAKES 6–8 SERVINGS

1 Prepare and chill the dough as directed.

2 In a frying pan, melt 1 tablespoon of the butter over medium heat. Add the chopped leeks and cook, stirring frequently, until tender, about 10 minutes. Transfer to a bowl.

3 Add the remaining 1 tablespoon butter to the pan and melt over medium heat. Add the mushrooms and cook, stirring occasionally, until the juices evaporate and the mushrooms begin to brown, about 8 minutes. Return the leeks to the pan. Stir in the cream and thyme and bring to a boil over high heat. Cook, stirring frequently, until the cream is almost evaporated, about 3 minutes. Transfer to a bowl, stir in the cheese, and season with salt and pepper. Let cool completely.

4 Preheat the oven to 375°F (190°C). Cut a piece of parchment paper to fit a 16-by-12-inch (40-by-30-cm) rimmed baking sheet. Turn the baking sheet over, and place the parchment on the underside. Roll out the puff pastry on a floured work surface into an 16-by-12-inch (40-by-30-cm) rectangle about ⅛ inch (3 mm) thick. Transfer the dough to the parchment paper. Refrigerate the dough on the baking sheet for 15 minutes.

5 Remove the pastry from the refrigerator. Slide the pastry (with the parchment) onto a work surface. Trim the rough edges of the pastry. Spoon the mushroom mixture in a vertical 3-inch (7.5-cm) strip down the center of the pastry, leaving a 1-inch (2.5-cm) border at the top and bottom. Using the tip of a small sharp knife and cutting toward the filling on the diagonal, cut strips 1 inch (2.5 cm) wide along the side of the pastry, stopping where the cut reaches the mushroom mixture. Fold the strips of dough diagonally, alternating left and right, over the filling. Tuck the ends underneath. Carefully slide the pastry with the parchment back onto the underside of the baking sheet. Refrigerate for 15 minutes.

6 Remove the pastry from the refrigerator. Lightly brush the top of the pastry with some of the beaten egg. Bake until the braid is puffed and golden brown, 35–40 minutes. Let cool for 10 minutes. Cut the braid crosswise into thick slices, transfer to a large platter, and serve warm.

variation Use mixed wild mushrooms instead of just cremini. You can also substitute Cheddar for the fontina cheese.

GRILLED POLENTA
WITH BLACK BEAN SALSA

Kosher salt

1⅓ cups (9½ oz/295 g)
coarse-ground polenta

1 can (15 oz/485 g)
black beans, drained
and rinsed

1 large ripe tomato,
seeded and diced

½ cup (3 oz/90 g) fresh or
thawed frozen corn kernels

¼ cup (1½ oz/45 g)
minced yellow onion

3 tablespoons chopped
fresh cilantro

1 tablespoon fresh
lime juice

1 hot fresh green chile,
such as jalapeño or
serrano, seeded
and minced

1 clove garlic, minced

1 tablespoon olive oil

½ cup (2½ oz/75 g)
crumbled *queso fresco* or
feta cheese for serving

MAKES 6 SERVINGS

Black bean tamales are one of my favorite snacks at my local farmers' market. But the multi-step method of stuffing, rolling, and steaming requires more time and attention than I usually have available. This dish—which features thick wedges of polenta and an easy-to-prepare chile, corn, and black bean salsa—is a tasty alternative.

1 To make the polenta, in a large, heavy saucepan, bring 5⅓ cups (43 fl oz/1.3 l) water and 1½ teaspoons salt to a boil over medium-high heat. Gradually whisk in the polenta. Reduce the heat to medium-low and cover. Cook, whisking frequently, until the polenta is thick and creamy, about 45 minutes. Add up to ½ cup (4 fl oz/125 ml) water by tablespoons if the polenta begins to stick to the bottom of the pan. (Be careful as the hot polenta can splatter.)

2 Lightly oil a 9-by-13-inch (23-by-33-cm) baking dish. Spread the polenta in the dish. Cover the polenta with parchment or waxed paper and refrigerate until firm and cold, at least 1½ hours or up to overnight. (This can be done the night before serving.)

3 To make the black bean salsa, stir the beans, tomato, corn, onion, cilantro, lime juice, chile, and garlic in a bowl. Season with salt. Cover and let stand to blend the flavors, at least 30 minutes.

4 Preheat the broiler. Have ready a rimmed baking sheet. Cut the polenta crosswise into 6 rectangles, and brush the tops with half of the olive oil. Using a wide spatula, transfer the polenta pieces to the baking sheet, oiled sides down. Brush with the remaining olive oil. Place in the broiler about 6 inches (15 cm) from the heat source. Broil, turning once, until both sides are golden, about 5 minutes per side.

5 Cut each rectangle into 3 triangles. Arrange 3 triangles on each plate, and top with the bean salsa, dividing it evenly. Sprinkle with the cheese and serve at once.

variations Pinto beans can stand in for the black beans. You can also substitute Spicy Black Beans with Chorizo (page 184) for the salsa.

SWEET 16TH - A BAKERY NASHVILLE, TN

There are some baked goods that just seem to taste best when the scent of your first cup of coffee fills the air—muffins, coffee cake, scones, and Danish, to name a few. Sweet 16th in East Nashville offers wonderful versions of these goodies and more. The pocket-sized spot is owned and operated by Ellen and Dan Einstein, self-taught bakers with a passion that shows in every morsel that goes out their door. There are a few seats available so you can sit and linger over your selection, being sure to get every last crumb. While sweets are the main draw, their savory dishes are also extraordinary, such as their always-popular Grittata. You would search far and wide to find a tastier breakfast casserole than this one, sporting cheesy grits topped with vegetables and light custard. Be sure to use aged provolone, which has a sharper flavor than the regular or smoked varieties. This hearty, comforting dish is perfect for a crowd—plus, it can be made ahead of time and then reheated in the oven just before serving.

"GRITTATA"

BREAKFAST CASSEROLE

½ cup (4 oz/125 g) unsalted butter

1 cup (8 fl oz/250 ml) heavy cream

20 cloves garlic, minced

Salt and freshly ground pepper

1½ cups (9 oz/280 g) quick-cooking grits

2½ cups (10 oz/315 g) shredded aged provolone cheese

12 large eggs

2 cups (16 oz/500 g) thinly sliced oil-packed sun-dried tomatoes, undrained

24 green onions, white and green parts, chopped

1 large portobello mushroom, cap and stem trimmed and chopped

¼ cup (2 fl oz/60 ml) whole milk

MAKES 12 SERVINGS

1 Preheat the oven to 350°F (180°C). Lightly oil a 9-by-13-inch (23-by-33-cm) baking dish. In a heavy, large saucepan, melt the butter over medium heat. Add 1 quart (32 fl oz/1 l) water, the cream, garlic, 2 teaspoons salt, and 2 teaspoons pepper and bring to a boil over high heat. Gradually whisk in the grits. Reduce the heat to medium-low and cook, whisking frequently, until thick and creamy, about 6 minutes. Whisk in 1 cup (4 oz/125 g) of the cheese.

2 In a bowl, whisk 4 of the eggs. Gradually whisk in 2 cups (16 fl oz/500 ml) of the cooked grits. Pour into the saucepan with the remaining grits, return to medium-low heat, and whisk until lightly thickened, about 1 minute more. Spread the mixture evenly in the prepared dish. Place the dish on a rimmed baking sheet. Bake until the grits feel set when pressed with your fingers, about 12 minutes.

3 Meanwhile, place the sun-dried tomatoes and their oil in a large frying pan. Cook over medium heat until the oil is heated, about 1 minute. Add the green onions and mushroom and cook, stirring often, just until the green onions are wilted and tender, about 6 minutes.

4 Remove the baking dish from the oven. Spread the green onion mixture evenly over the grits. In a bowl, whisk together the remaining 8 eggs and the milk. Pour slowly and evenly over the vegetables. Sprinkle with the remaining 1½ cups (6 oz/185 g) cheese. The dish will be very full. Bake until the top is golden brown, about 35 minutes. Remove from the oven and let stand for 10 minutes. Cut into portions and serve hot. (The dish can be made ahead, cooled, covered, and refrigerated for up to 2 days. Reheat, covered with aluminum foil, in a 350°F/180°C oven until heated through, about 40 minutes.)

variation If you don't want to make such a large portion, you can cut the ingredients in half and bake the casserole in an 8-inch (20-cm) square baking dish.

CORN SPOONBREAD

WITH CHEDDAR AND BACON

3 thick slices
applewood-smoked bacon,
coarsely chopped

3 cups (24 fl oz/750 ml)
whole milk

Kosher salt and
freshly ground pepper

1 cup (7 oz/220 g)
yellow cornmeal,
preferably stone-ground

4 tablespoons (2 oz/60 g)
unsalted butter,
cut into small pieces

3 large eggs, separated

1 cup (4 oz/125 g) shredded
sharp Cheddar cheese

1 cup (6 oz/185 g) fresh or
thawed frozen corn kernels

2 green onions, white
and pale green parts,
finely chopped

Chopped fresh chives
for garnish (optional)

MAKES 6 SERVINGS

A cross between a soufflé and cornbread, spoonbread is one of the glories of Southern cuisine. My version combines a handful of breakfast favorites into one dish: the eggy cornmeal pudding is enhanced with crumbles of bacon, a sprinkling of sharp Cheddar, and kernels of fresh corn. You'll get some of each in every delicious spoonful.

1 Preheat the oven to 375°F (190°C). In a large frying pan, fry the bacon over medium heat, stirring frequently, until crisp and golden, about 6 minutes. Using a slotted spoon, transfer to paper towels to drain. Discard the fat in the pan.

2 In a large saucepan over medium-high heat, bring 2 cups (16 fl oz/500 ml) of the milk, 1½ teaspoons salt, and ¼ teaspoon pepper to a boil, being careful that the milk does not boil over. Gradually whisk in the cornmeal and return to a boil. Reduce the heat to medium-low and cook, whisking frequently, until the cornmeal is quite thick, about 2 minutes.

3 Remove from the heat. Add the butter and whisk until melted. In a bowl, whisk together the remaining 1 cup (8 fl oz/250 ml) milk and the egg yolks and whisk into the cornmeal mixture. Stir in the cheese, corn, and green onions. Set aside.

4 In a clean bowl, beat the egg whites with a handheld mixer on high speed until soft peaks form. Stir about one-fourth of the whites into the cornmeal mixture to lighten it, then fold in the remaining whites. Butter a 2-quart (2-l) baking dish or six 1½-cup (12-fl oz/375-ml) individual baking dishes. Spread the cornmeal mixture evenly in the prepared dish(es).

5 Bake until puffed and golden brown, about 25 minutes for the large spoonbread and 15–20 minutes for the individual spoonbreads. Garnish with chives, if using, and serve at once.

variation You can spice this up by substituting pepper jack for the Cheddar. Or, add 1 or 2 roasted, peeled, and chopped poblano chiles to the mixture before folding in the egg whites.

CHEESE SOUFFLÉ
WITH FRESH CHIVES

2 tablespoons unsalted
butter, plus more
for greasing

3 tablespoons freshly
grated Parmesan cheese

3 tablespoons
all-purpose flour

1 cup (8 fl oz/250 ml)
whole milk, warmed

1 cup (4 oz/125 g) shredded
Gruyère or Comté cheese

2 tablespoons chopped
fresh chives

Kosher salt and
freshly ground pepper

4 large eggs, separated,
plus 1 large egg white,
at room temperature

MAKES 4 SERVINGS

I will forever be thankful to the French chef who taught me how to make a cheese soufflé. It's easier to make than you think, and it transforms simple breakfast ingredients—eggs and cheese—into an ethereal treat. Serve the soufflé right after baking to show off its dramatic height, but don't worry if it starts to fall a bit—it will still taste delicious.

◇◇◇

1 Preheat the oven to 375°F (190°C). Butter a 2-quart (2-l) soufflé dish, sprinkle with the Parmesan cheese, and tilt to coat the sides evenly; leave any loose cheese in the dish.

2 In a saucepan, melt the 2 tablespoons butter over medium heat. Whisk in the flour. Reduce the heat to medium-low and let bubble for 1 minute without browning. Gradually whisk in the milk, raise the heat to medium, and bring to a boil, whisking frequently. Reduce the heat to medium-low and cook, whisking frequently, until very thick, about 3 minutes. Remove from the heat. Whisk in the cheese and chives. Stir in ¼ teaspoon salt and ¼ teaspoon pepper. The mixture will be sticky.

3 In a large bowl, whisk the egg yolks until blended. Gradually whisk the warm cheese mixture into the yolks. In another bowl, using a handheld mixer on high speed, beat the 5 egg whites until soft peaks form. Stir about one-fourth of the beaten egg whites into the yolk mixture to lighten it, then gently fold in the remaining whites just until combined. Pour into the prepared dish. Insert a butter knife into the soufflé mixture and trace a circle about 1 inch (2.5 cm) deep and 1 inch (2.5 cm) from the sides of the dish. (This helps create a "crown" in the soufflé.)

4 Bake until the soufflé is puffed and golden brown and it quivers gently when jostled (the insides will be lightly set and maybe a bit soft), about 25 minutes. Serve at once.

variation Shredded sharp Cheddar, Cantal, or crumbled goat cheese are all fine substitutes for the Gruyère.

HERB-INFUSED
PARMESAN CUSTARD

Butter for the ramekins

¾ cup (3 oz/90 g) freshly
grated Parmesan cheese

2 cups (16 fl oz/500 ml)
half-and-half

1 teaspoon minced
fresh thyme

1 clove garlic, minced

3 large eggs, plus
4 large egg yolks

Kosher salt and freshly
ground white pepper

MAKES 4 SERVINGS

This eggy custard has just a touch of garlic, for a piquant, but not too brash, flavor. I like to serve it as the centerpiece of a brunch, with a tangle of mixed greens on the side. I also like to present it in tandem with vegetables such as grilled asparagus spears, or a saucy ragout such as Spanish Piperade with Ham and Smoked Paprika (page 169).

1 Preheat the oven to 325°F (165°C). Lightly butter six ¾-cup (6-fl oz/ 180-ml) ramekins or custard cups, sprinkle with the Parmesan cheese, and tilt to coat the sides evenly; tap out and reserve the excess cheese. Arrange the ramekins in a baking dish just large enough to hold them.

2 In a saucepan, bring the half-and-half, minced thyme, and garlic to a simmer over medium-low heat. Remove from the heat, cover, and let stand for 5 minutes.

3 In a bowl, whisk together the eggs, yolks, ½ teaspoon salt, and ¼ teaspoon white pepper until blended. Gradually whisk the warm half-and-half mixture into the yolks, then whisk in the reserved cheese. Pour into a glass measuring cup or pitcher. Divide evenly among the prepared ramekins.

4 Place the baking dish with the ramekins on the oven rack. Gently pull out the rack and pour enough hot water into the baking dish to come about ½ inch (12 mm) up the sides of the ramekins. Gently push the oven rack back into place. Bake until a butter knife inserted into a ramekin comes out clean, 30–35 minutes. Remove the baking pan from the oven, then use tongs to remove the ramekins from the water. Serve at once.

SNOOZE, AN A.M. EATERY DENVER, CO

With three locations in the Denver area (and a fourth location in Fort Collins to the north), Snooze's mission is to "re-energize" the breakfast experience, and it begins the second you walk in the door: Start with a vibrant, Jetsons-meets–Happy Days design aesthetic. Add a menu that is as playful as the décor, taking familiar favorites and reinventing them with creativity and flair, such as breakfast pot pie, pineapple upside-down pancakes, s'mores French toast, and a Bugs Bloody (a Bloody Mary with a shot of carrot juice). Finish with an entertaining, efficient, and knowledgeable waitstaff, and you'll see why customers keep coming back for seconds. Corned beef hash is often made from the leftovers of a corned beef dinner, but this outstanding version, from Snooze Eatery chef Scott Bermingham, proves that it's very much worth making from scratch, just for the breakfast table. The poblano chile gives the hash extra pizzazz. Serve the crispy hash cakes with Homemade Ketchup (page 212)—which, by the way, is also worth making from scratch.

CORNED BEEF HASH
WITH CARAMELIZED ONIONS AND CHILES

1 corned beef brisket,
about 2⅓ lb (1.2 kg)

1 teaspoon whole cloves

1 teaspoon yellow
mustard seed

1 teaspoon
black peppercorns

1 teaspoon coriander seed

2 bay leaves

1 large russet potato,
about 12 oz (375 g),
scrubbed but unpeeled

2 tablespoons olive oil

1 small yellow
onion, chopped

1 poblano chile, seeded
and chopped

Kosher salt and freshly
ground pepper

2 tablespoons
unsalted butter

12 Poached or Fried Eggs
(page 211)

MAKES 6 SERVINGS

1 Rinse the corned beef and put it in a large Dutch oven or a heavy pot. Add enough cold water to cover by 1 inch (2.5 cm). Bring to a boil over medium-high heat, skimming off any foam that rises to the surface. Add the cloves, mustard seed, peppercorns, coriander seed, and bay leaves. Reduce the heat to medium-low, cover, and simmer gently until almost tender, 2½–3 hours.

2 Add the potato to the pot and return the liquid to a simmer. Cook until the brisket and potato are fully tender, about 30 minutes longer. Transfer the corned beef and potato to a carving board and let cool completely. (The corned beef and potato can be prepared, covered, and refrigerated, up to 1 day ahead.)

3 Slice the corned beef across the grain, trimming any excess fat. Coarsely chop enough corned beef to measure 2½ cups (15 oz/470 g). Save the remaining corned beef for another use. Peel the cooked potato and shred it on the large holes of a box grater-shredder. In a food processor fitted with the chopping blade, pulse the corned beef and potatoes until the beef is finely chopped.

4 Meanwhile, in a heavy, large frying pan, preferably cast iron, heat 1 tablespoon of the oil over medium-low heat. Add the onion and cook, stirring frequently, until caramelized and golden brown, 15–20 minutes. Transfer the onion to a bowl.

5 Heat the remaining 1 tablespoon oil in the frying pan over medium heat. Add the chile and cover. Cook, uncovering to stir occasionally, until tender, about 6 minutes. Add the chile and onions to the beef mixture and mix. Season with salt and pepper.

6 In the same frying pan, melt the butter over medium heat. Divide the corned beef mixture into 6 portions, and shape each portion into a thick patty. Place the patties in the pan and press them gently with a metal spatula. Cook until the undersides are crisp and browned, about 5 minutes. Using the spatula, flip the patties over, press gently with the spatula, and cook until the other sides are browned, about 5 minutes more.

7 Place each patty on a plate or in a shallow bowl and top each serving with 2 poached or fried eggs. Serve at once.

SPICY VEGGIE HASH

WITH SWEET POTATOES, PEPPERS, AND CORN

1½ lb (750 g) orange-
fleshed sweet potatoes,
peeled and
cut into small cubes

1½ lb (750 g) Yukon gold
potatoes, peeled and cut
into small cubes

2 tablespoons olive oil

1 medium yellow
onion, chopped

1 red bell pepper,
seeded and chopped

1 jalapeño chile, seeded
and minced

1 cup (6 oz/185 g) fresh or
thawed frozen corn kernels

1½ teaspoons
ground cumin

3 tablespoons chopped
fresh cilantro,
plus more for garnish

Kosher salt and freshly
ground pepper

Plain yogurt for serving

Lime wedges for serving

MAKES 4–6 SERVINGS

Until recently, I was a naysayer of vegetable-only hash.
I happily ate my words, however, when a friend convinced
me to develop this Mexican-inspired hash, loaded with
two types of potatoes, sweet peppers, chiles, corn, and
a hit of fragrant cumin and cilantro. A squeeze of fresh
lime juice and a dollop of creamy yogurt enhance the
flavors of the dish.

1 Preheat the oven to 400°F (200°C). Lightly oil a large rimmed baking
sheet. Place all of the potatoes on the sheet and toss with 1 tablespoon
of the oil. Roast for 30 minutes. Using a metal spatula, turn the potatoes,
and continue roasting until lightly browned and tender, about 15 minutes
longer. Keep warm.

2 Meanwhile, in a large frying pan, heat the remaining 1 tablespoon oil
over medium heat. Add the onion, bell pepper, and jalapeño. Cook, stirring
occasionally, until the vegetables are tender, about 10 minutes. Stir in the
corn and cook until heated through, about 3 minutes. Stir in the cumin and
cook until fragrant, about 30 seconds. Add the sweet potatoes, Yukon gold
potatoes, and 3 tablespoons cilantro and stir to combine. Season with salt
and pepper.

3 Divide the hash among individual bowls, topping each serving with a dollop
of yogurt and a sprinkle of cilantro. Serve at once, with the lime wedges.

variation If you wish, top each serving of hash with a poached or
fried egg (page 211).

CLASSIC CHICKEN HASH
WITH MIXED FRESH HERBS

1³/₄ lb (875 g) skin-on, bone-in chicken breasts

2 cups (16 fl oz/500 ml) Chicken Stock (page 214) or low-sodium chicken broth

1 small yellow onion, sliced

Kosher salt and freshly ground pepper

1¹/₂ lb (750 g) russet potatoes, scrubbed but unpeeled

7 tablespoons (3¹/₂ oz/ 105 g) unsalted butter

1 red bell pepper, seeded and chopped

3 tablespoons minced shallots

3 tablespoons all-purpose flour

2 tablespoons heavy cream

2 teaspoons minced fresh rosemary

2 teaspoons minced fresh sage

Chopped fresh chives for garnish

MAKES 4–6 SERVINGS

1 In a large saucepan, combine the chicken breasts, stock, onion, ¹/₂ teaspoon salt, and ¹/₄ teaspoon pepper. Add enough cold water to barely cover the chicken. Bring to a boil over high heat. Reduce the heat to medium-low and simmer until the chicken shows no sign of pink when pierced with a sharp knife, about 30 minutes. Transfer to a carving board and let stand until cool enough to handle. Strain the stock through a wire sieve and measure 1¹/₂ cups (12 fl oz/375 ml); set aside. Reserve the remaining stock for another use; discard the onion. Remove and discard the skin and bones from the chicken. Cube the meat and transfer to a bowl.

2 Meanwhile, put the potatoes in another saucepan and add enough salted water to cover. Bring to a boil over high heat. Reduce the heat to medium-low, cover, and simmer until the potatoes are tender when pierced with the tip of a sharp knife, about 25 minutes. Drain and rinse under cold running water. Let the potatoes stand until cool enough to handle, then peel and cube. Add to the chicken.

3 In a large frying pan, preferably nonstick, melt 2 tablespoons of the butter over medium heat. Add the bell pepper and cook, stirring frequently, until tender, about 5 minutes. Add the shallots and cook until tender, about 2 minutes more. Add to the chicken and potatoes.

4 In a saucepan, melt 3 tablespoons of the butter over medium-low heat. Whisk in the flour and let bubble for 1 minute without browning. Gradually whisk in the 1¹/₂ cups reserved stock, raise the heat to medium, and bring to a boil, whisking frequently. Reduce the heat to medium-low and cook, whisking frequently, until reduced by about one-third, 8–10 minutes. Stir in the cream. Add to the chicken mixture, along with the rosemary and sage, and stir well, breaking up the potatoes with the side of the spoon. Season with salt and pepper.

5 Wipe out the frying pan with paper towels. Add the remaining 2 tablespoons of butter to the pan and melt over medium-high heat. Add the chicken mixture, and press it into a flat disk with a metal spatula. Cook until browned and crusty, 4–5 minutes. Using the spatula, turn sections of the hash over (it should not remain whole), and press down again. Cook until the second side is browned, 4–5 minutes more.

6 Divide among individual bowls, sprinkling each serving with chives. Serve at once.

RED FLANNEL HASH
WITH BACON

2 beets (about ¾ lb/375 g), scrubbed and trimmed

2 russet potatoes, scrubbed but unpeeled

Kosher salt and freshly ground pepper

6 thick slices applewood-smoked bacon, coarsely chopped

1 yellow onion, chopped

½ cup (4 oz/125 g) sour cream, plus more for serving

1 tablespoon minced fresh dill, plus more for serving

Canola oil for cooking, if needed

MAKES 4 SERVINGS

Red flannel hash often incorporates leftover ingredients from a hearty corned beef supper, with beets staining the dish their signature red color. My version includes crispy bacon and fresh dill. The beets can be roasted the night before for faster assembly in the morning.

1 Preheat the oven to 400°F (200°C). Wrap each beet in aluminum foil. Place on a baking sheet and bake until just tender when pierced with the tip of a sharp knife, about 1 hour, depending on the age of the beets. Unwrap the beets and let cool until easy to handle. Slip off the skins and cut the beets into cubes. Transfer to a bowl.

2 Meanwhile, put the potatoes in a large saucepan and add enough salted water to cover. Bring to a boil over high heat. Reduce the heat to medium-low, cover, and simmer until the potatoes are tender when pierced with the tip of a sharp knife, about 25 minutes. Drain and rinse under cold running water. Let stand until cool enough to handle. Peel and cut into cubes, then add to the beets.

3 In a frying pan, fry the bacon over medium heat, stirring, until crisp and golden, about 6 minutes. Using a slotted spoon, transfer to paper towels to drain. Pour out and reserve the bacon fat.

4 Return 1 tablespoon of the bacon fat to the frying pan and heat over medium heat. Add the onion and cook, stirring frequently, until tender, about 3 minutes. Transfer the onions to the bowl with the beets and potatoes, along with the bacon, ½ cup sour cream, and 1 tablespoon dill. Using a wooden spoon, stir well to combine, breaking up the beets and potatoes with the side of the spoon. Season with salt and pepper.

5 Return 2 tablespoons of the bacon fat to the frying pan (add canola oil, if needed) and heat over medium heat. Add the beet mixture and press it into a flat disk with a metal spatula. Cook until browned and crusty, 4–5 minutes. Using the spatula, turn sections of the hash over (it should not remain whole) and press down again. Cook until the second side is browned, 4–5 minutes longer.

6 Divide among individual bowls, topping each serving with a dollop of sour cream and a sprinkle of dill. Serve at once.

SPANISH PIPERADE
WITH HAM AND SMOKED PAPRIKA

1 tablespoon olive oil

3 oz (90 g) serrano ham, Bayonne ham, or prosciutto, finely diced

1 red bell pepper, seeded and cut into strips

1 green bell pepper, seeded and cut into strips

2 cloves garlic, minced

4 large ripe tomatoes, seeded and diced (about 3 cups/18 oz/560 g)

1 teaspoon Spanish smoked or sweet paprika

Kosher salt and freshly ground pepper

Chopped fresh flat-leaf parsley for garnish

4 Fried or Poached Eggs (page 211), optional

MAKES 4 SERVINGS

Piperade, tender sweet peppers cooked with cured ham and enlivened with smoked paprika and garlic, is a typical Basque dish. But you'll find it to be a versatile breakfast staple: Make a batch and watch it disappear, tucked into an omelet, heaped onto toasted bread, or spooned into a bowl and topped with a fried or poached egg.

1 In a frying pan, heat the oil over medium heat. Add the ham and cook, stirring frequently, until lightly browned, about 3 minutes. Add the bell peppers and cook, stirring occasionally, until the peppers are tender, 6–8 minutes. Stir in the garlic and cook until it softens, about 1 minute.

2 Stir in the tomatoes and cook until they give off some of their juices, about 3 minutes. Reduce the heat to medium-low and cover. Cook, stirring occasionally, until the vegetables are very tender, 20–25 minutes.

3 Uncover the pan and stir in the paprika. Continue to cook until the juices thicken, about 5 minutes. Season with salt and pepper. Divide among individual bowls, topping each serving with some parsley and a fried or poached egg, if desired. Serve hot, warm, or at room temperature.

variation It's hardly traditional, but diced salami makes a great substitute for the ham.

NEW ORLEANS–STYLE
BBQ SHRIMP AND GRITS

Grits

1⅓ cups (8 oz/250 g) stone-ground white corn grits (not quick-cooking)

1⅓ cups (11 fl oz/330 ml) whole milk

Kosher salt

6 tablespoons (3 oz/90 g) unsalted butter, cut into tablespoons

BBQ Shrimp

1½ lb (750 g) medium shrimp, peeled and deveined

1 cup (8 fl oz/250 ml) dark beer, preferably Abita

¼ cup (2 fl oz/60 ml) Worcestershire sauce

2 tablespoons hot pepper sauce, such as Crystal or Tabasco

1 tablespoon fresh lemon juice

1 teaspoon minced fresh rosemary

1 tablespoon unsalted butter, chilled

MAKES 4 SERVINGS

1 To make the grits, place the grits in a large bowl and add enough cold water to cover by 1 inch (2.5 cm). Let stand for 5 minutes. Skim off any bran or hulls floating on the surface of the water. Drain the grits in a fine-mesh sieve. In a large heavy saucepan, bring 1 quart (32 fl oz/1 l) water, the milk, and 2 teaspoons salt to a boil over high heat. Gradually whisk in the grits. Reduce the heat to low and simmer, whisking every 5 minutes, until the grits are thick and tender, about 45 minutes. Remove from the heat and whisk in the 6 tablespoons butter, one tablespoon at a time.

2 About 10 minutes before the grits are done, make the shrimp. Heat a large frying pan over medium-high heat. Add the shrimp and cook until one side is seared, about 1 minute. Transfer the shrimp to a bowl.

3 Add the beer, Worcestershire sauce, hot sauce, and lemon juice to the frying pan and deglaze the pan, scraping the bottom with a wooden spoon to dislodge any browned bits. Cook, stirring frequently, until reduced by about one-third, about 5 minutes. Return the shrimp to the pan and cook until they turn opaque throughout, about 1 minute more. Remove from the heat and stir in the rosemary. Add the 1 tablespoon butter and stir until melted and the sauce is lightly thickened (the sauce will still be thin).

4 Divide the grits evenly among 4 bowls. Top with equal amounts of the shrimp and sauce. Serve at once.

THE RUBY SLIPPER CAFE NEW ORLEANS, LA

The Ruby Slipper Cafe was founded by Erich and Jennifer Weishaupt, a local couple who, like Dorothy from the Wizard of Oz, truly believe there is no place like home. Their cozy corner location in the heart of New Orleans' Mid-City neighborhood is off the well-beaten tourist trail and caters to local folks. The menu abounds with Louisiana specialties such as crab cakes, as well as many dishes invented in New Orleans, such as eggs Sardou (named after a visiting French dramatist) and *pain perdu* with bananas Foster (a name which honors a restaurateur's close friend). And since the city is known for its love of a good cocktail, even at breakfast, the cafe mixes up several quintessential Crescent City eye-openers, including brandy milk punch and a house-made Bloody Mary. In The Ruby Slipper's version of the favorite southern dish of "barbecued" shrimp (so-named even though it doesn't touch a grill), fresh local shrimp is bathed in a tangy mixture of beer and Worcestershire sauce and served over creamy grits for a uniquely New Orleans breakfast.

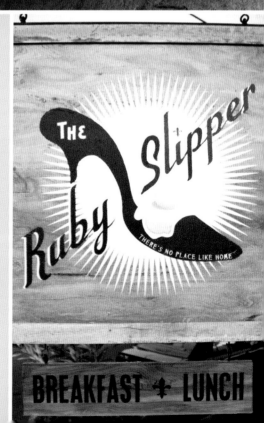

5

ON THE SIDE

MAPLE-GLAZED BACON
WITH CRACKED BLACK PEPPER

12 thick slices
applewood-smoked bacon

2 tablespoons
pure maple syrup

½ teaspoon coarsely
ground black pepper

MAKES 6 SERVINGS

Those who surreptitiously drizzle a little extra maple syrup off to the side of their pancakes understand the maple-bacon love affair. This recipe is a dangerous combination of those sweet, salty, and crunchy elements that render it completely addictive. It's so easy to make that after trying it, you may never want plain-old bacon again.

1 Preheat the oven to 400°F (200°C). Spread the bacon out in a single layer on a large rimmed baking sheet.

2 Bake until the bacon is barely crisp and browned, 15–20 minutes. Carefully drain off and discard the fat from the baking sheet.

3 Brush 1 tablespoon of the maple syrup over the bacon strips and sprinkle with half of the pepper. Return to the oven and bake until glazed and shiny, about 2½ minutes. Remove from the oven and, using tongs, flip the bacon slices over. Brush the other sides with the remaining 1 tablespoon syrup and sprinkle with the remaining pepper. Bake again until glazed and shiny, about 2 minutes more. Transfer the bacon to a serving platter. Let stand 2–3 minutes (the bacon will firm up and become extra-crispy). Serve warm.

variation You can use honey in place of the maple syrup. You can also experiment with different kinds of peppers (such as white or Sichuan) or chile powders (such as cayenne or chipotle).

PORK AND SAGE
SAUSAGE PATTIES

2 tablespoons
dried bread crumbs

2 teaspoons minced
fresh sage or 1 teaspoon
dried sage

1 teaspoon minced
fresh rosemary or
½ teaspoon dried rosemary

1 teaspoon minced
fresh thyme or
½ teaspoon dried thyme

¼ teaspoon
red pepper flakes

Pinch of ground cloves

Pinch of freshly
grated nutmeg

Kosher salt and
freshly ground
black pepper

1½ lb (750 g) ground pork

1 tablespoon
pure maple syrup

MAKES 6 SERVINGS

I rarely buy link pork sausage anymore, since I much prefer the flavor of my own herb-flecked patties. For the freshest, brightest flavor, when your herb garden is going full tilt, pluck the classic seasonings of rosemary, sage, and thyme. A small amount of bread crumbs soaks up and holds in the juices, which helps keep the sausage meat naturally moist.

1 In a large bowl, stir together the bread crumbs, sage, rosemary, thyme, red pepper flakes, cloves, nutmeg, 1¾ teaspoons salt, and ½ teaspoon black pepper. Add the ground pork and maple syrup. Mix gently with your hands until just combined. Cover and refrigerate for 30–45 minutes.

2 Shape the pork mixture into 6 patties about 3 inches (7.5 cm) in diameter. Heat a large frying pan, preferably nonstick, over medium heat. Add the patties and reduce the heat to medium-low. Cook until the bottoms are browned, about 5 minutes. Flip and cook the other sides until browned and the centers of the patties feel firm when pressed with your finger, about 5 minutes more. Serve hot.

variation Try substituting half of the ground pork with ground beef round. Add a small clove of garlic, minced, if you'd like.

HAM STEAKS
WITH RED-EYE GRAVY

1 tablespoon
unsalted butter

1 smoked ham steak
(about 1¼ lb/625 g)

¾ cup (6 fl oz/180 ml)
brewed coffee
(not dark roast)

1 teaspoon sugar

MAKES 4 SERVINGS

An old Southern favorite, this classic dish combines the drippings from fried ham steaks with brewed coffee and a little sugar to make an eye-opening gravy. The gravy is meant to be thin, so resist gussying it up with a roux or other thickeners. Serve this dish with fried eggs, cheesy grits, and plenty of warm, freshly baked biscuits for sopping up the gravy.

1 In a large frying pan, melt the butter over medium-high heat. Add the ham and cook until the bottom is browned, about 3 minutes. Flip and cook the other side until browned, about 2 minutes more. Transfer the ham to a platter and cover with foil to keep warm. Pour out all but 1 tablespoon fat from the pan.

2 Add the coffee and sugar to the pan and deglaze the pan over high heat, scraping the bottom with a wooden spoon to dislodge any browned bits. Cook until the liquid is reduced by about half (it will be thin "gravy"), about 3 minutes. Remove from the heat.

3 Cut the ham into 4 portions and divide among individual plates. Drizzle the ham with the gravy and serve at once.

variation In the South, this dish is made with country ham, which is salt-cured and smoked. You can also make this dish with smoked pork chops.

O'BRIEN-STYLE
HASH BROWNS

1 lb (500 g) strawberries, hulled and sliced

3 tablespoons granulated sugar

1 package (2 1/4 teaspoons) active dry yeast

1/4 cup (2 fl oz/60 ml) warm (105°–115°F/40°–46°C) water

1 1/4 cups (10 fl oz/310 ml) whole milk

1/2 cup (4 fl oz/125 ml) sparkling water

1/2 cup (4 oz/125 g) unsalted butter, melted and cooled

4 large eggs, separated

1 teaspoon pure vanilla extract

2 1/2 cups (12 1/2 oz/390 g) all-purpose flour

1/2 teaspoon fine sea salt

Canola oil for cooking, if needed

Confectioners' sugar for serving

Sweetened Whipped Cream (page 216) for serving

MAKES 4 SERVINGS

The secret to crisp hash browns is to remove as much moisture as possible from the potatoes before cooking them. Both Boston and New York claim the invention of potatoes O'Brien, which includes a colorful accent of chopped green or red bell pepper and onion.

1 In a heavy frying pan, preferably cast iron, melt the butter over medium heat. Add the onion and bell pepper and cook, stirring occasionally, until tender, about 10 minutes. Season with salt and pepper. Transfer to a bowl and set aside.

2 Using a food processor fitted with the shredding attachment or the large holes of a box grater-shredder, shred the potatoes. A handful at a time, press the potatoes in a potato ricer to remove as much moisture as possible. Place the potatoes in a large bowl. Add 1 1/2 teaspoons salt and 1/4 teaspoon pepper and mix well.

3 In the frying pan, heat 2 tablespoons of the oil over medium heat until it shimmers. Add the potato mixture and spread into a thick cake. Reduce the heat to medium, cover, and cook until the underside is golden brown and crisp, about 6 minutes. Using a wide metal spatula, transfer the potatoes to a plate. Add the remaining oil to the pan and heat. Flip the potatoes back into the pan, browned side up. Continue cooking, uncovered, until the potatoes are golden brown and crisp on the other side, about 6 minutes more.

4 Slide the potatoes onto a platter. Return the onion mixture to the frying pan and cook, stirring often, until reheated, about 1 minute. Heap the onion mixture onto the potatoes. Serve at once.

PAPAS FRITAS

WITH SANTA FE–STYLE CHILE SAUCE

About 2 cups (16 fl oz/ 500 ml) Cafe Pasqual's Red Chile Sauce (page 214) or Green Chile Sauce (page 213), or 1 cup (8 fl oz/250 ml) of each

4½ lb (2.25 kg) medium red potatoes, scrubbed but unpeeled

Kosher salt and freshly ground pepper

½ cup (4 fl oz/125 ml) Clarified Butter (page 212) or canola oil

2 teaspoons sweet paprika

1½ cups (6 oz/185 g) shredded Monterey jack cheese

⅔ cup (5½ oz/170 g) sour cream, at room temperature

4 green onions, white and pale green parts, thinly sliced, for serving

MAKES 6 SERVINGS

1 Prepare the red and/or green chile sauce(s) as directed.

2 Put the potatoes in a large pot and add enough cold salted water to cover. Bring to a boil over high heat. Reduce the heat to medium-low, cover, and simmer until the potatoes are tender when pierced with the tip of a sharp knife, 20–25 minutes. Drain and rinse under cold running water. Let stand until cool enough to handle. Slice the potatoes into rounds about ½ inch (12 mm) thick. (The potatoes can be prepared up to 1 day ahead, covered, and refrigerated.)

3 Preheat the oven to 200°F (95°C). In a large frying pan, preferably cast iron, heat ¼ cup (2 fl oz/60 ml) of the clarified butter over medium-high heat. Add half of the potatoes and cook, stirring occasionally, until golden brown, about 12 minutes. Transfer to a rimmed baking sheet and keep warm in the oven while frying the remaining potatoes in the remaining butter. Combine the two batches in the frying pan. Sprinkle with the paprika, season with salt and pepper, and stir to combine.

4 Preheat the broiler. Have ready another rimmed baking sheet. Divide the potatoes evenly among 6 heatproof bowls or serving dishes. Top each with about ⅓ cup (3 fl oz/80 ml) of the red or green sauce, then ¼ cup (1 oz/30 g) of the cheese. Arrange the bowls on the baking sheet and broil until the cheese is melted and bubbling, about 1 minute. Top each serving with a dollop of sour cream and a scattering of green onions. Serve at once.

variation For a complete meal (not that this isn't substantial on its own), top each serving with some cooked Mexican chorizo sausage or a fried egg (page 211).

CAFE PASQUAL'S SANTA FE, NM

Named for the folk saint of Mexican and New Mexican kitchens, Cafe Pasqual's serves unsurpassable versions of Southwestern food, with a focus on fresh—and mostly organic—ingredients. Housed in a historic pueblo-style adobe located in downtown Santa Fe, and festively decorated with colorful Mexican tiles, hand-painted murals, and strings of dried chile peppers, the restaurant truly reflects its surroundings. Owner Katharine Kagel's expansive menu includes favorites like *huevos rancheros*, breakfast burritos, and *papas fritas*, crispy potatoes doused in a red or green chile sauce, covered in melted cheese, and served with a flour or corn tortilla. If you can't decide between the two chile sauces, order your potatoes "Christmas-style" for some of each. At home, you can make either sauce, or both, as they freeze well. And you'd better be hungry, because this recipe makes generous portions. If you can, fry the potatoes in clarified butter, which imparts a buttery flavor but won't burn over higher heat levels like regular butter.

ROASTED ROOT VEGETABLES
WITH FRESH THYME

4 Yukon gold potatoes
(about 1½ lb/750 g), peeled
and cut into cubes

2 parsnips
(about ½ lb/250 g), peeled
and cut into cubes

2 large carrots,
peeled and cut into cubes

1 celery root, peeled and
cut into cubes

3 tablespoons olive oil

2 yellow onions, cut
lengthwise into quarters

1½ teaspoons minced
fresh thyme

Kosher salt and
freshly ground pepper

MAKES 6–8 SERVINGS

Naturally sweet roasted root vegetables are a delicious counterpoint to the smoky and salty flavors of crisp bacon or sliced ham. With the exception of beets, which will stain other ingredients, use any combination of cubed vegetables you like, from crispy-edged potatoes to sweet carrots and parsnips to earthy celery root.

1 Preheat the oven to 425°F (220°C). Lightly oil a large roasting pan. In a large bowl, toss the potatoes, parsnips, carrots, and celery root with 2 tablespoons of the oil to coat. Spread in the prepared pan. Bake until the vegetables begin to soften, about 25 minutes.

2 Toss the onion wedges with the remaining 1 tablespoon oil, trying to keep the wedges intact. Remove the roasting pan from the oven and turn the vegetables over with a metal spatula. Nestle the onion wedges among the vegetables in the pan. Continue roasting until the vegetables are very tender and their edges are tinged dark brown, about 25 minutes more.

3 Sprinkle the roasted vegetables with the thyme, season with salt and pepper, and toss gently. Serve at once.

variation To glaze the root vegetables, drizzle them with 3 tablespoons pure maple syrup during the last 5 minutes of roasting, and turn to coat.

SPICY BLACK BEANS
WITH CHORIZO

1 tablespoon olive oil

4 oz (125 g) fresh
Mexican-style chorizo
sausage, casings removed

1 yellow onion, chopped

1 red bell pepper,
seeded and diced

1 jalapeño chile,
seeded and minced

1 clove garlic, minced

2 cans (15 oz/485 g each)
black beans,
drained and rinsed

½ cup (4 fl oz/125 ml)
Chicken Stock (page 214) or
low-sodium chicken broth

3 tablespoons chopped
fresh cilantro or oregano

Sour cream for serving
(optional)

MAKES 4–6 SERVINGS

Chorizo lends deep flavor to these nourishing beans, perfect for spooning alongside Mexican-inspired breakfast dishes such as Texas-Style Migas with Ranchero Sauce (page 52) or Chilaquiles with Tomatillo Salsa and Eggs (page 59). The beans are also great on their own, topped with sour cream or shredded Cheddar cheese and accompanied by warm tortillas.

1 In a medium saucepan, heat the oil over medium-high heat. Add the chorizo and cook, breaking up the chorizo with the side of a wooden spoon, until it begins to brown, about 8 minutes.

2 Add the onion, bell pepper, jalapeño, and garlic, and reduce the heat to medium. Cook, stirring frequently, until the onion is tender, about 5 minutes. Add the beans and stock. Bring to a simmer. Reduce the heat to medium-low and simmer until the liquid is reduced by half, about 15 minutes.

3 Using the side of a large spoon, crush some of the beans in the saucepan to thicken the juices. Stir in 2 tablespoons cilantro. Spoon onto plates or into bowls and garnish with the remaining 1 tablespoon cilantro and a dollop of sour cream, if desired. Serve at once.

CHEESE GRITS

WITH BACON AND GREEN ONIONS

1 tablespoon
unsalted butter

1 clove garlic, minced

1 cup (8 fl oz/250 ml)
whole milk

Kosher salt

1 cup (7 oz/220 g)
white hominy grits,
preferably stone-ground

3 thick slices
applewood-smoked bacon,
coarsely chopped

1 cup (4 oz/125 g) shredded
sharp Cheddar cheese

½ cup (2 oz/60 g) freshly
grated Parmesan cheese

Hot pepper sauce

2 green onions, white and
green parts, minced

MAKES 6 SERVINGS

Grits, one of the great ambassadors of Southern food, are more than just a plain side dish for eggs. They can be served in a multitude of ways; my favorite is with bacon, onions, and cheese mixed right in. If you prefer, you can cook the grits, covered, in the top part of a double boiler set over simmering water (to help keep the grits from sticking to the pot).

1 In a heavy saucepan, melt the butter over medium heat. Add the garlic and cook, stirring often, until the garlic softens and is fragrant, about 1 minute. Add 3 cups (24 fl oz/750 ml) water, the milk, and 1 teaspoon salt and bring to a boil over high heat. Gradually whisk in the grits and bring to a simmer. Reduce the heat to low and simmer, whisking every 5 minutes, until thick and tender, about 45 minutes.

2 Meanwhile, in a frying pan, fry the bacon over medium heat, stirring, until crisp and golden, about 6 minutes. Using a slotted spoon, transfer to paper towels to drain.

3 When the grits are done, stir in the Cheddar and Parmesan cheeses, the bacon, and the green onions. Season to taste with hot pepper sauce and salt. Serve at once.

variation For even cheesier grits, you can substitute shredded Monterey jack cheese for the Parmesan.

CINNAMON TOAST

WITH BUTTER AND HONEY

¼ cup (2 oz/60 g)
unsalted butter,
at room temperature

2 teaspoons mild honey

1 teaspoon
ground cinnamon

8 slices good-quality
white sandwich bread

MAKES 8 SLICES

The scent of cinnamon always seems to evoke happy memories of comforting breakfasts. This is a childhood classic that's too good to skimp on ingredients: make your toast with bakery-fresh bread, luscious European-style butter, and fragrant, high-quality cinnamon. For the sweet accent, I prefer to use honey rather than granulated sugar.

1 Preheat the broiler. Have ready a rimmed baking sheet. In a small bowl, using a fork or rubber spatula, mash together the butter, honey, and cinnamon.

2 Arrange the bread on the baking sheet. Broil until the bread is toasted, about 1 minute. Remove from the broiler and flip the bread over. Spread equal amounts of the cinnamon butter over the untoasted sides of the bread. Return to the broiler and broil until the cinnamon butter is bubbling and the edges of the bread are toasted, about 1 minute. Serve hot.

variation Whole wheat bread is every bit as good as white sandwich bread. You can also use your favorite artisan bread, as long as it doesn't have too many holes in it, which will allow the butter to leak through.

BUTTERMILK
ANGEL BISCUITS

2½ cups (12½ oz/390 g)
all-purpose flour

2 tablespoons sugar

1 teaspoon baking powder

½ teaspoon baking soda

½ teaspoon fine sea salt

1 teaspoon quick-rise yeast

¼ cup (2 oz/60 g)
unsalted butter,
cut into cubes, chilled,
plus room temperature
butter for serving

¼ cup (2 oz/60 g)
vegetable shortening,
cut into cubes, chilled

1 cup (8 fl oz/250 ml)
buttermilk

Honey or Quick Strawberry
Jam (page 102) for serving

MAKES 10 BISCUITS

These "angel" biscuits owe their light, airy texture to the use of multiple leaveners in the dough. I make these often, usually in a big batch. The dough can be refrigerated for a couple of days, so you can bake fresh biscuits, a few at a time, whenever you want them. Cutting the dough into squares instead of rounds eliminates scraps.

1 In a bowl, sift together the flour, sugar, baking powder, baking soda, and salt. Stir in the yeast. Using a pastry blender or 2 knives, cut the butter and shortening into the flour mixture just until the mixture forms coarse crumbs about the size of peas. Add the buttermilk to the dry ingredients and stir with a fork or rubber spatula just until combined.

2 Shape the dough into a ball. Lightly butter a large bowl. Add the dough and turn to coat with the butter. Cover the bowl tightly with plastic wrap. Let the dough rise in a warm spot until it doubles in bulk, about 1¼ hours. (The dough can be refrigerated for up to 2 days before baking. After the dough is made, shape into a thick disk, close in a zippered plastic bag, and refrigerate. Punch down every 12 hours or so. Remove from the refrigerator 1 hour before patting it out.)

3 Preheat the oven to 425°F (220°C). Line a baking sheet with parchment paper. Punch down the dough, then turn out onto a floured work surface. Pat into a 10-by-5-inch (25-by-13-cm) rectangle about ¾ inch (2 cm) thick. Cut into ten 2-inch (5-cm) squares. Place 1 inch (2.5 cm) apart on the prepared baking sheet. Bake until golden brown, 17–20 minutes. Serve the biscuits warm with butter and honey.

HIGH-RISE BISCUITS
WITH SAUSAGE GRAVY

Sausage Gravy

¼ lb (125 g) bulk
pork breakfast sausage

2 tablespoons
unsalted butter,
melted, or as needed

¼ cup (1½ oz/45 g) *each*
finely chopped yellow
onion and green
bell pepper

¼ cup (1½ oz/45 g)
all-purpose flour

2¼ cups (18 fl oz/560 ml)
Chicken Stock (page 214) or
chicken broth, warmed

⅔ cup (5 fl oz/160 ml)
heavy cream

Kosher salt and
freshly ground pepper

Hot pepper sauce

Biscuits

2 cups (10 oz/315 g)
Southern-style soft wheat
flour (such as White Lily), or
1 cup (5 oz/155 g) *each*
all-purpose and cake flour

1 tablespoon
baking powder

1 teaspoon sugar

½ teaspoon fine sea salt

2 tablespoons each
unsalted butter and
vegetable shortening,
cut into cubes, chilled

1 tablespoon lard,
cut into cubes, chilled

¾ cup (6 fl oz/180 ml)
buttermilk

MAKES 4–6 SERVINGS

1 To make the gravy, heat a frying pan over medium heat. Add the sausage and cook, stirring and breaking it up with the side of a wooden spoon, until it is browned, about 6 minutes. With a slotted spoon, transfer the sausage to a bowl. Measure the fat in the pan and add enough melted butter to make 3 tablespoons. (The amount depends on the fat content of the sausage.) Add the onion and bell pepper and cook, stirring frequently, until softened, about 3 minutes. Return the sausage to the pan. Sprinkle with the flour and stir well. Reduce the heat to low and let simmer, stirring frequently, without browning, 1–2 minutes. Gradually whisk in the warmed chicken stock and bring to a boil over high heat. Reduce the heat to medium-low and simmer, stirring frequently, until lightly thickened, about 10 minutes. Stir in the cream. Return to a boil over high heat, reduce the heat to medium-low, and simmer, stirring frequently, until the gravy is reduced to about 3 cups (24 fl oz/750 ml), about 15 minutes. Season to taste with salt, pepper, and hot pepper sauce. Cover and keep the gravy warm over very low heat.

2 Meanwhile, make the biscuits. Preheat the oven to 425°F (220°C). Have ready a rimmed baking sheet. In a bowl, sift together the flour, baking powder, sugar, and salt. Using a pastry blender or 2 knives, cut the butter, shortening, and lard into the flour mixture just until the mixture forms coarse crumbs about the size of peas. Pour in the buttermilk and stir with a fork or rubber spatula just until combined.

3 Turn out the dough onto a floured surface. Knead just until the dough comes together, about 10 strokes. Using floured hands, pat into a circle about 1 inch (2.5 cm) thick. Using a 2-inch (5-cm) biscuit cutter dipped in flour, cut out as many rounds of the dough as possible. Gather up the scraps, knead briefly, and continue patting and cutting out to make 6–8 biscuits. Place on the rimmed baking sheet without touching. Bake until golden brown, 15–17 minutes. Let cool on the baking sheet for 3 minutes. Serve the biscuits on individual plates, topped with the warm gravy.

HOMINY GRILL CHARLESTON, SC

A Southern breakfast is often built on the foundation of biscuits, grits, and sausage gravy. It's a challenge to sell stalwarts like these in the South, as so many diners will make comparisons to Grandma's homemade recipe. But Hominy Grill, a beloved Charleston restaurant that's housed in a former barbershop, need not fear. Chef-proprietor Robert Stehling cooks traditional Southern specialties that taste just like Grandma used to make (assuming she was the best cook in town). Grandma would know that the very best hominy grits are stone-ground, and that they are so good they deserve to have a restaurant named for them. She'd also know that pork lard can be the key to fine biscuits, and that fresh, local eggs make all the difference. Stehling utilizes these culinary secrets and more, and the result is some of the best breakfasts south of the Mason-Dixon line. Hominy Grill's version of high-rise biscuits and sausage gravy—with buttermilk, lard, and soft wheat flour in the biscuits, and careful simmering of the gravy—is Southern to the core.

CHEESE AND CHILE
SKILLET CORNBREAD

2 poblano chiles

1 cup (5 oz/155 g) all-purpose flour

1 cup (7 oz/220 g) yellow cornmeal, preferably stone-ground

2 teaspoons baking powder

½ teaspoon fine sea salt

¼ cup (2 oz/60 g) unsalted butter

¾ cup (6 fl oz/180 ml) whole milk

¼ cup (3 oz/90 g) pure maple syrup

1 large egg, beaten

1 cup (4 oz/125 g) shredded sharp Cheddar cheese

1 cup (6 oz/185 g) fresh or thawed frozen corn kernels

MAKES 8 SERVINGS

This not-too-sweet cornbread has earned a place at my breakfast table as the ultimate partner to scrambled eggs and spicy sausage. Gently sweetened with maple syrup and flecked with corn kernels, chunks of mild poblano chiles, and bits of sharp Cheddar cheese, then baked in a cast-iron skillet, it isn't your everyday cornbread.

1 Preheat the broiler. Place the chiles on a baking sheet and broil, turning occasionally, until the skins are blackened on all sides, about 12 minutes. Transfer to a cutting board and let cool until easy to handle. Peel off the blackened skin. Discard the stem, seeds, and ribs, and chop the chiles.

2 Preheat the oven to 400°F (200°C). In a bowl, sift together the flour, cornmeal, baking powder, and salt. Make a well in the center of the flour mixture.

3 Place the butter in a 10-inch (25-cm) heatproof frying pan, preferably cast iron. Place in the oven until the butter is melted, about 3 minutes. Remove the pan from the oven and pour 2 tablespoons of the melted butter into a large bowl, leaving the remaining butter in the pan and tilting the pan to coat. Add the milk, maple syrup, and egg to the butter in the bowl and stir to combine. Pour the milk mixture into the well in the flour mixture and stir just until combined. Fold in the chopped chile, cheese, and corn. Spread the batter in the hot pan.

4 Bake until the cornbread is golden brown and a toothpick inserted into the center comes out clean, about 30 minutes. Transfer to a wire rack and let cool in the pan for 5 minutes. Cut into wedges and serve hot or warm.

CARAMELIZED ONION ROLLS
WITH ASIAGO CHEESE

3½ cups (17½ oz/545 g)
bread flour, or as needed

1 package (2¼ teaspoons)
quick-rise yeast

2 tablespoons olive oil

1½ teaspoons fine sea salt

1½ cups (7½ oz/235 g)
chopped yellow onions

Kosher salt and
freshly ground pepper

½ cup (4 oz/125 g) plus
2 tablespoons freshly
grated Asiago cheese

MAKES 12 ROLLS

These rolls are stuffed with sweet caramelized onions and pungent Asiago cheese. A peek of filling shows through the top of each roll, and hints at what's inside. If you wish, bake the rolls in oiled muffin cups for a more tailored look.

1 In a small bowl, stir together ½ cup (2½ oz/75 g) of the flour, ¼ teaspoon of the yeast, and ½ cup (4 fl oz/125 ml) cold water. Cover the bowl tightly with plastic wrap. Let stand in a warm spot until bubbling, 20–30 minutes.

2 Scrape the yeast mixture into the bowl of a stand mixer fitted with the paddle attachment. Add 1 cup (8 fl oz/250 ml) water, 1 tablespoon of the oil, and the remaining 2 teaspoons yeast. With the mixer on medium-low speed, add the salt and remaining flour as needed to make a soft, sticky dough that does not stick to the bowl. Remove the paddle attachment and fit the stand mixer with the dough hook attachment. Knead the dough on medium-low speed until soft and supple, 5–7 minutes.

3 Shape the dough into a ball. Lightly oil a large bowl. Add the dough and turn to coat with the oil. Cover the bowl tightly with plastic wrap. Let the dough rise in a warm spot until it doubles in bulk, about 1¼ hours. Or refrigerate overnight until doubled in size, at least 6 or up to 12 hours. Remove from the refrigerator 1 hour before shaping the rolls.

4 Meanwhile, in a frying pan, heat the remaining 1 tablespoon oil over medium heat. Add the onions and reduce the heat to medium-low. Cook, stirring frequently, until the onions are golden brown and tender, about 20 minutes. Transfer to a bowl and let cool completely. Season with salt and pepper. Stir in the cheese.

5 Punch down the dough and turn it out onto a floured work surface. Cut the dough into 12 equal portions and shape each into a ball. Working with one ball at a time, roll out the dough into a 4–5-inch (10–13-cm) round about ½ inch (12 mm) thick. Place a heaping teaspoon of the filling in the center of each round. Bring up the edges of the round to meet in the center, and pinch the seams to seal. Transfer, seam side down, to a baking sheet, spacing the rolls about 1 inch (2.5 cm) apart. Cover with plastic wrap and let rise in a warm spot until doubled in bulk, about 45 minutes.

6 Preheat the oven to 400°F (200°C). Using kitchen scissors, snip an X at the top of each roll to expose the filling. Bake until the rolls are golden and the bottoms sound hollow when rapped, about 20 minutes. Let cool for at least 10 minutes before serving.

SAVORY CHEESE PUFFS

WITH GRUYÈRE AND BLACK PEPPER

½ cup (4 oz/125 g)
unsalted butter,
cut into cubes

½ cup (4 fl oz/125 ml)
whole milk

½ teaspoon coarsely
ground pepper

¼ teaspoon fine sea salt

1 cup (5 oz/155 g)
all-purpose flour

5 large eggs

½ cup (2 oz/60 g)
shredded Gruyère cheese

MAKES ABOUT 24 PUFFS

These airy cheese puffs are a relative of the popover, leavened only by eggs to expand in the heat of the oven. Called *gougères* in French, they are often served as hors d'oeuvres, but also make a delicious and elegant accompaniment to a fluffy omelet, a simple green salad, and a glass of sparkling wine for a late-morning brunch.

1 Preheat the oven to 400°F (200°C). Line a rimmed baking sheet with parchment paper. In a medium, heavy saucepan, bring the butter, milk, ½ cup (4 fl oz/125 ml) water, the pepper, and salt to a boil over medium heat, checking that the butter is melted by the time the water boils. All at once, add the flour and stir well with a wooden spoon until the mixture comes together in a mass. Reduce the heat to medium-low and stir until the mixture begins to film the bottom of the saucepan, about 1 minute. Remove from the heat and let cool for 3 minutes. Transfer to a large bowl.

2 In a small bowl, beat together 4 of the eggs. Using a handheld mixer on medium speed, gradually beat the eggs into the flour mixture, letting the first addition be absorbed before adding another. Using a spoon, stir in the cheese. The dough will be very sticky.

3 Spoon the dough into a pastry bag fitted with a ½-inch (12-mm) plain tip. Pipe about 24 small mounds, spacing them about 1 inch (2.5 cm) apart, onto the prepared baking sheet. In a small bowl, beat the remaining egg. Brush the top of each dough mound, smoothing the peak on the top as you do so. Bake, without opening the oven door, until puffed and golden, about 25 minutes.

4 Remove the pan from the oven. Quickly pierce the side of each cheese puff with the tip of a small sharp knife to allow air to escape. Return to the oven and bake until crisp and golden brown, 5–10 minutes longer. Let cool on the baking sheet for 5 minutes. Serve warm or at room temperature.

CLASSIC POPOVERS

WITH FRUIT JAM

1 cup (5 oz/155 g)
all-purpose flour

½ teaspoon fine sea salt

1 cup (8 fl oz/250 ml)
whole milk

2 large eggs, at room
temperature, beaten

¼ cup (2 oz/60 g)
unsalted butter, melted,
plus room temperature
butter for serving (optional)

Apricot or peach jam
for serving

MAKES 12 POPOVERS

If more people knew how utterly easy they are to make, feather-light popovers would be served at every meal. Their crusty surfaces and hollow interiors are the perfect medium for warm butter and your favorite fruit jam or preserves. They will puff up during baking, but don't worry too much if they deflate; they're best served hot, straight from the oven.

1 Preheat the oven to 450°F (230°C). Have ready a standard 12-cup muffin pan. In a bowl, whisk together the flour and salt. Make a well in the center of the flour mixture and add the milk and eggs. Whisk just until combined. Pour the batter into a glass measuring cup or a pitcher.

2 Place the muffin pan in the oven and heat until hot, about 2 minutes. Remove from the oven and spoon 1 teaspoon of the melted butter into each cup. Divide the batter evenly among the muffin cups, filling them half-full.

3 Bake for 10 minutes. Reduce the heat to 375°F (190°C) and continue baking, without opening the oven door, until the popovers are puffed, crisp, and golden brown, 20–25 minutes. Using your fingers, gently remove the piping-hot popovers from the pan and serve at once with the jam and butter, if desired.

variation For savory popovers, add 2 teaspoons minced fresh rosemary or thyme and ½ teaspoon freshly ground pepper to the batter.

CRISPY CORN FRITTERS
WITH FRESH CILANTRO

Canola oil for deep-frying

1½ cups (7½ oz/235 g) all-purpose flour

2 teaspoons baking powder

1 teaspoon fine sea salt

1 cup (8 fl oz/250 ml) whole milk

2 large eggs, beaten

1 cup (6 oz/185 g) fresh or thawed frozen corn kernels

2 tablespoons minced yellow onion

2 tablespoons minced fresh cilantro

MAKES ABOUT 24 FRITTERS

My brothers and I were amazed the first time we saw our father make corn fritters. Peering into the pot—from a safe distance—we watched the dough rounds puff and turn golden-brown in the hot oil. To our family recipe, I've added cilantro and onions, for a slightly Indian flavor.

1 Pour oil to a depth of at least 3 inches (7.5 cm) into a large, heavy saucepan, preferably cast iron, and heat over high heat to 350°F (180°C) on a deep-frying thermometer. Preheat the oven to 200°F (95°C). Place a wire rack over a rimmed baking sheet and place near the stove.

2 While the oil is heating, in a bowl, sift together the flour, baking powder, and salt. Make a well in the center of the flour mixture. In a separate bowl, whisk together the milk and eggs and pour into the well in the flour mixture. Stir just until combined. Gently fold in the corn, onion, and cilantro.

3 In batches to avoid crowding, add tablespoonfuls of the batter to the hot oil. Deep-fry the fritters until golden brown, turning once at the halfway point, about 3 minutes. Using a wire skimmer or a metal slotted spoon, transfer to the rack and keep warm in the oven while you fry the remaining fritters. Serve at once.

variation For Dad's fritters (see headnote), omit the onions and cilantro. Serve the fritters with maple syrup.

HONEY-GLAZED ROASTED PEACHES
WITH MASCARPONE

½ cup (4 oz/125 g)
mascarpone cheese

3 tablespoons heavy cream

¼ teaspoon
ground cinnamon

4 ripe peaches,
preferably freestone, pitted
and halved lengthwise

2 tablespoons melted butter

2 tablespoons honey,
slightly warmed until liquid

MAKES 4 SERVINGS

Roasting coaxes the juices from peaches, creating an appealingly messy, sweet treat, especially when topped with decadent mascarpone. The tart flavor of the peaches matches well with salty meats such as sausage, bacon, and ham. Or, chop up the roasted peaches and serve them over oatmeal or stacks of buttermilk pancakes.

1 Preheat the oven to 400°F (200°C). In a small bowl, mix together the mascarpone, cream, and cinnamon with a rubber spatula. Set aside and let stand at room temperature while roasting the peaches.

2 Have ready a baking dish just large enough to hold the peach halves in a single layer. Butter the dish with 1 tablespoon of the melted butter. Place the peaches in the dish, cut side up, and brush the halves with the remaining 1 tablespoon melted butter.

3 Bake until the peach juices collect in the hollows where the pits were removed, about 15 minutes. Remove from the oven. Brush the peaches with the honey, letting the juices run into the baking dish. Return to the oven and bake until the peaches are tender, about 5 minutes more. Serve the peaches at once, with the cooking juices spooned on top, and topped with the cinnamon mascarpone.

variation Grill the buttered peach halves over medium heat for 5 minutes, then brush them with the warm honey and grill until tender, about 2 minutes more.

DRINKS

THE PERFECT CUP OF COFFEE

12 tablespoons (5 oz/155 g) freshly ground
coffee beans (coarsely ground if using
a French press; medium-fine ground if using drip)

6 cups (48 fl oz/1.5 l) just-boiled filtered water

Sugar and milk or half-and-half for serving

1 If using a French press, measure the coarsely
ground coffee into the pot. Pour in the just-boiled
water. Place the lid on the pot with the strainer
just touching the top of the water. If you have
a French press cozy, place it over the pot to keep
the coffee hot as it brews. Let the coffee steep for
4–6 minutes, depending on how strong you prefer
your brew. Then slowly push down the strainer
as far as it will go to trap the grounds at the bottom.

2 If making drip coffee, place a filter-lined cone
over a drip pot and measure the medium-fine-ground
coffee into the filter. Very slowly pour in the just-
boiled water through the filter, allowing the water
to drain into the pot before adding more. Serve the
coffee at once with sugar and milk.

MAKES 4–6 SERVINGS

VANILLA ICED COFFEE

1 cup (7 oz/210 g) freshly ground coffee

1 cup (8 fl oz/250 ml) whole milk

¼ cup (2 oz/60 g) sugar, or to taste

4 vanilla beans, split lengthwise

Ice cubes

1 In a pitcher or large bowl, stir the ground
coffee into 4 cups (32 fl oz/1 l) cold or room
temperature water. Cover and let sit overnight
at room temperature.

2 In a saucepan over medium heat, combine
the milk and sugar. Using the tip of a small knife,
scrape the seeds from the vanilla beans into the
mixture and then add the pods. Bring the mixture

to a simmer and immediately remove from the
heat. Allow to steep for about 20 minutes.
Strain the milk mixture through a fine-mesh sieve
into a measuring pitcher.

3 Select 4 tumblers. Strain the coffee through
a fine-mesh sieve into a large bowl. Strain again
through a coffee filter into a large, clean pitcher.
Fill the glasses with ice cubes. Pour the coffee
into the glasses, filling them to within 1 inch
(2.5 cm) of the rim. Top each glass with ¼ cup
(2 fl oz/60 ml) of the vanilla-flavored milk.
Serve at once.

MAKES 4 SERVINGS

CAFÉ MOCHA

2 tablespoons unsweetened cocoa powder

1 tablespoon sugar

1 cup (8 fl oz/250 ml) brewed double-strength coffee

2 cups (16 fl oz/500 ml) whole milk

1 Select 2 large mugs. In a saucepan, combine
the cocoa powder, sugar, and coffee, and heat
over medium heat until hot and steaming, about
5 minutes. Remove from the heat. Divide evenly
between the mugs.

2 If you have an espresso machine, steam and
froth the milk according to the manufacturer's
instructions. Pour the hot milk into the mugs and
top with milk foam. Alternatively, in a saucepan,
warm the milk over medium-high heat until small
bubbles appear around the edge of the pan.
Do not allow the milk to boil. Pour the hot milk
into the mugs and stir to combine. Serve at once.

MAKES 2 SERVINGS

HOT CHOCOLATE

4 cups (32 fl oz/1 l) whole milk

5 oz (155 g) finely chopped bittersweet chocolate

2–4 tablespoons sugar

2 cinnamon sticks (optional)

Sweetened Whipped Cream (page 216) or marshmallows for garnish (optional)

1 Select 4 small cups or mugs. In a saucepan over medium-low heat, combine the milk, chocolate, sugar to taste, and cinnamon sticks, if using. Cook, stirring to dissolve the sugar, until bubbles form around the edges of the pan. Do not allow the milk to boil.

2 Discard the cinnamon sticks, if using, and whisk the mixture until it is hot and frothy. Pour the hot chocolate into the mugs and garnish each with whipped cream or marshmallows, if desired. Serve at once.

variation To make Mexican hot chocolate, use 4 wedges (3 oz/90 g each) Mexican chocolate, chopped, in place of the bittersweet chocolate, sugar, and cinnamon.

MAKES 4 SERVINGS

THE PERFECT POT OF TEA

6 cups (48 fl oz/1.5 l) just-boiled filtered water

2 tablespoons plus 1 teaspoon loose tea leaves such as green tea, black tea, or herbal tea

Milk, sugar cubes or honey, and lemon slices for serving

1 Pour a small amount of boiling water into a teapot, swirl it around, put the lid in place, and let the water sit in the pot for about 1 minute to warm it. Pour out the water.

2 Add the tea leaves to the pot and fill the pot with the just-boiled water. Put the lid in place. If you have a tea cozy, place it over the pot to keep the tea hot as it brews. Let green tea steep for 1–3 minutes, black tea for 3–6 minutes, and herbal tea for 8–12 minutes. Stir the leaves briefly, then pour the tea through a small strainer into warmed cups.

3 Set out the milk, sugar, and lemon slices for guests to add to their cups as desired. Serve at once.

MAKES 4–6 SERVINGS

CHAI LATTE

2 cinnamon sticks

16 cardamom pods

16 whole cloves

4 peppercorns

10 thin slices peeled fresh ginger

2–4 tablespoons sugar

2 tablespoons plus 2 teaspoons Darjeeling tea leaves

1⅓ cups (11 fl oz/330 ml) whole milk

1 Select 4 mugs. In a saucepan, combine the cinnamon sticks, cardamom pods, cloves, peppercorns, ginger slices, and 3 cups (24 fl oz/750 ml) water. Bring to a boil over medium heat, cover, reduce the heat to low, and simmer until the liquid becomes aromatic, about 10 minutes.

2 Add sugar to taste and bring to a simmer over medium heat. Stir in the tea leaves, remove from the heat, cover, and let steep until the chai is the desired strength, 3–5 minutes.

3 Meanwhile, if you have an espresso machine, steam and froth the milk according to the manufacturer's instructions. Alternatively, in a saucepan, bring the milk to a simmer over medium heat. Pour the hot milk into the mugs, dividing it evenly. Pour the chai through a tea strainer or fine-mesh sieve into the mugs, dividing it evenly. Serve at once.

MAKES 4 SERVINGS

FRUIT SMOOTHIE

2 ripe bananas, peeled and frozen

2 cups (12 oz/375 g) pineapple, peach, or mango cubes, frozen

1 cup (4 oz/125 g) raspberries, blueberries, or hulled and sliced strawberries, frozen

1/2 cup (4 oz/125 g) vanilla yogurt

1 1/2 cups (12 fl oz/375 ml) orange juice

1 Select 4 tumblers. In a blender, combine the bananas, cubed fruit, berries, yogurt, and orange juice and process until thick and creamy. Taste and adjust the flavor if necessary with more fruit, yogurt, or juice. Divide between the glasses. Serve at once.

MAKES 4 SERVINGS

MANGO LASSI

2 ripe mangoes

1 teaspoon fresh lemon juice

2–4 tablespoons sugar or honey

2 cups (16 oz/500 g) nonfat plain yogurt

1 cup (8 oz/250 g) ice cubes

1 To cut the mangoes, stand each fruit on one of its narrow sides, with the stem end facing you. Using a sharp knife, and positioning it about 1 inch (2.5 cm) from the stem, cut down the length of the fruit, just brushing the large, lengthwise pit. Repeat the cut on the other side of the pit. One at a time, holding each half cut side up, score the flesh in a grid pattern, forming 1/4-inch (6-mm) cubes and stopping just short of the skin. Push against the skin side to force the cubes outward, then cut across the base of the cubes to free them.

2 Select 4 tall glasses. In a blender, combine the mangoes, lemon juice, sugar to taste, yogurt, and ice. Blend until frothy and smooth. Divide between the glasses and serve at once.

MAKES 4 SERVINGS

STRAWBERRY AGUA FRESCA

5 cups (1 1/4 lb/625 g) hulled strawberries, plus strawberry slices for garnish

1/2 cup (4 oz/125 g) sugar

1/3 cup (3 fl oz/80 ml) fresh lime juice

Coarse sea salt

Ice cubes

1 Select 4 tumblers. In a blender, combine half of the strawberries and 1 1/2 cups (12 fl oz/375 ml) water and purée until smooth. Place a fine-mesh sieve over a bowl. Pour the purée into the sieve, using a silicone spatula to press the mixture through the sieve. Discard the strawberry seeds left in the sieve. Repeat with the remaining strawberries and 1 1/2 cups (12 fl oz/375 ml) more water.

2 Pour the strained strawberry purée into a pitcher. Stir in the sugar, lime juice, and 1/4 teaspoon salt. Add up to 2 cups (16 fl oz/500 ml) more water to reach the desired consistency. To serve, fill the glasses with ice. Divide the agua fresca between the glasses, garnish with strawberry slices, and serve at once.

MAKES 4 SERVINGS

HONEYDEW AGUA FRESCA

2 honeydew melons, halved and seeded

Juice of 4 lemons

3/4 cup (6 oz/185 g) sugar

1 cup (1 oz/30 g) crushed fresh mint leaves

3 cups (24 fl oz/750 ml) sparkling water, chilled

3 lemons, thinly sliced

Ice cubes

1 Using a metal spoon, scoop out the melon flesh into a large bowl. Working in batches, purée the melon in a blender or food processor. As each batch is finished, transfer it to another large bowl. Add the lemon juice, sugar, and mint leaves to the purée and stir to combine until the sugar is fully dissolved.

Cover the bowl and let stand at room temperature for at least 1 hour or up to 4 hours to blend the flavors.

2 When ready to serve, pour the melon mixture through a medium-mesh sieve into a large pitcher or jar. Add the sparkling water, lemon slices, and ice and stir well. Ladle or pour the agua fresca into glasses and serve at once.

MAKES 10–12 SERVINGS

SPARKLING RASPBERRY LEMONADE

1 cup (8 oz/250 g) sugar

2 lemon peel strips, plus 6 lemon slices for garnish

1 cup (4 oz/125 g) raspberries

¾ cup (6 fl oz/180 ml) fresh lemon juice

1½ bottles (48 fl oz/1.5 l) sparkling water, chilled

Ice cubes

1 Select 6 tumblers. In a saucepan, combine the sugar, 1 cup (8 fl oz/250 ml) water, the lemon peel strips, and raspberries. Bring to a boil over medium heat, stirring to dissolve the sugar and break up the raspberries, and boil for 1 minute. Remove from the heat and let cool, stirring occasionally to infuse the sugar syrup with raspberry flavor. Strain the syrup through a fine-mesh sieve into a small pitcher or bowl. Stir in the lemon juice and refrigerate until cold.

2 Just before serving, transfer the syrup mixture to a pitcher or a punch bowl, add the sparkling water, and stir well. Add ice cubes. Divide evenly among the tumblers and garnish each serving with a lemon slice. Serve at once.

MAKES 6 SERVINGS

MIMOSA

1 cup (8 fl oz/250 ml) fresh orange juice or blood orange juice, chilled

4 tablespoons (2 fl oz/60 ml) orange liqueur (optional)

1 bottle (24 fl oz/750 ml) Champagne, Prosecco, or dry sparkling wine, chilled

1 Select 4 Champagne flutes. Pour the orange juice into the flutes, dividing it evenly. Add 1 tablespoon orange liqueur, if using. Slowly fill the flutes with the Champagne. Stir briefly to blend the flavors. Serve at once.

MAKES 4 SERVINGS

GRAPEFRUIT CHAMPAGNE PUNCH

2 cups (16 fl oz/500 ml) fresh grapefruit juice

2 cups (16 fl oz/500 ml) fresh orange juice

½ cup (4 fl oz/125 ml) each fresh lemon juice and fresh lime juice

½ cup (3½ oz/105 g) superfine sugar

1 bottle (24 fl oz/750 ml) Champagne, Prosecco, or dry sparkling wine, chilled

4–5 teaspoons crème de cassis (optional)

1 In a large pitcher, combine the grapefruit, orange, lemon, and lime juices. Add the sugar and stir to dissolve completely. Refrigerate the pitcher until the juices are well chilled.

2 Select 8–10 Champagne flutes or stemmed glasses. Pour the Champagne into the pitcher and stir gently. Pour the punch into the glasses. Add ½ teaspoon of crème de cassis to each glass, if using (it will sink to the bottom of the glass). Serve at once.

MAKES 8–10 SERVINGS

PEACH BELLINI

2 ripe peaches, peeled, halved, and pitted

1 tablespoon superfine sugar, or to taste

1 teaspoon fresh lemon juice, or to taste

1 bottle (24 fl oz/750 ml) Champagne, Prosecco, or dry sparkling wine, chilled

1 Roughly chop the peaches. In a blender or food processor, process the peaches to a smooth purée. Taste and add sugar and/or lemon juice if needed; the purée should be sweet but not overly sweet.

2 Select 4 Champagne flutes. Fill each flute about one-third full with the peach purée. Slowly fill the flutes with the Champagne. Stir briefly to blend the flavors. Serve at once.

MAKES 4 SERVINGS

BALSAMIC BLOODY MARY

Ice cubes

1 cup (8 fl oz/250 ml) vodka

2 cups (16 fl oz/500 ml) tomato juice

1 tablespoon balsamic vinegar, preferably aged

2 teaspoons prepared horseradish

2 teaspoons Worcestershire sauce

Hot pepper sauce to taste

Juice of 1 lemon

Juice of 1 lime

Freshly ground pepper

4 celery stalks

4 each green olives and peperoncini

1 Select 4 tall glasses and fill with ice cubes. In a large pitcher, combine the vodka, tomato juice, vinegar, horseradish, Worcestershire sauce, hot pepper sauce, and lemon and lime juices. Season to taste with pepper and stir well to combine.

2 Pour the mixture into the glasses and garnish each glass with a celery stalk and a green olive and peperoncini speared onto a cocktail pick. Serve at once.

MAKES 4 SERVINGS

MICHELADA

1 tablespoon plus 1 teaspoon coarse sea salt

2 teaspoons pure chile powder

6 limes

Ice cubes

4 teaspoons Worcestershire sauce

Hot pepper sauce to taste

4 bottles (12 fl oz/375 ml each) Mexican beer such as Dos Equis or Pacifico

1 Select 4 tall glasses or tumblers. Spread the salt and chile powder on a small, flat plate. Cut 2 of the limes into 4 wedges each. Working with 1 glass at a time, run a lime wedge around the rim to moisten it and then dip the rim into the chile salt to coat it evenly. Repeat with the other glasses. Save 4 lime wedges for garnish.

2 Juice the remaining 4 limes; you should have about ½ cup (4 fl oz/125 ml) lime juice.

3 Fill each glass with several ice cubes. Add one-fourth of the lime juice, 1 teaspoon Worcestershire sauce, and a dash or two of hot pepper sauce to each glass. Pour 1 beer into each glass and stir gently. Garnish with a lime wedge and serve at once.

variation To make this more like a Bloody Mary, add a splash of tomato juice or Clamato to each drink.

MAKES 4 SERVINGS

BASIC RECIPES

SCRAMBLED EGGS

12 large eggs

Kosher salt and freshly ground pepper

2 tablespoons unsalted butter

1 In a bowl, whisk together the eggs, ¾ teaspoon salt, and ¼ teaspoon pepper just until thoroughly blended. Do not overbeat.

2 In a large frying pan, preferably nonstick, melt the butter over medium-low heat until the foam begins to subside. Add the egg mixture to the pan and cook until the eggs just begin to set, about 20 seconds. Stir with a heatproof spatula, scraping up the eggs on the bottom and sides of the pan and folding them toward the center. Repeat until the eggs are barely cooked into moist curds, about 3 minutes.

3 Remove the pan from the heat and let the eggs stand in the pan to allow the residual heat to finish cooking them, about 1 minute. Serve at once.

MAKES 4–6 SERVINGS

FRIED EGGS

2 tablespoons olive oil or unsalted butter

8 large eggs

Kosher salt and freshly ground pepper

1 In a large frying pan, preferably nonstick, heat 1 tablespoon of the oil over medium heat. One at a time, crack 4 of the eggs into the pan. Sprinkle the eggs with salt and pepper, cover, reduce the heat to medium-low, and cook until the whites begin to set and the yolks thicken, about 2 minutes for sunny-side-up eggs. Repeat with the remaining 1 tablespoon oil and 4 eggs. Serve at once.

2 To make over-easy, over-medium, or over-hard eggs, using a nonstick spatula, carefully flip the eggs and cook for about 30 seconds for eggs over easy,

about 1 minute for eggs over medium, and about 1½ minutes for eggs over hard.

note Start with cold eggs directly from the refrigerator. When cold, the yolks stay more intact and are less likely to break when you crack the eggs open.

MAKES 4 SERVINGS

POACHED EGGS

2 tablespoons distilled white vinegar

8 large eggs

1 In a wide saucepan, combine 8 cups (64 fl oz/2 l) water and the vinegar and bring to a boil. Fill a bowl halfway with hot tap water and place it near the stove. Reduce the heat to medium-low to keep the water at a simmer.

2 Crack an egg into a small bowl or ramekin. Slip the egg from the bowl into the simmering water. Using a large metal spoon, quickly spoon the egg white back toward the center of the egg to help the egg set in an oval shape. Simmer gently until the egg white is opaque and the egg is just firm enough to hold its shape, 3–4 minutes.

3 Using a slotted spoon, lift the egg out of the water. Trim off any floppy bits of white and carefully transfer the egg to the bowl of hot water. Repeat with the remaining eggs. With practice, you will be able to poach 2 or 3 eggs at the same time, but keep track of the order in which you add the eggs to the pan so you don't overcook any of them. The hot water will keep the eggs at serving temperature for up to 10 minutes.

note The fresher the eggs, the more attractive your poached eggs will be because the whites will form a neater, rounder shape. Check the date on the carton or, better yet, buy your eggs at the farmers' market.

MAKES 4 SERVINGS

CLARIFIED BUTTER

1 cup (8 oz/250 g) unsalted butter, cut into cubes

1 At least 4 hours before using, in a heavy saucepan, melt the butter over medium heat. Bring the butter to a boil. Reduce the heat to medium-low and simmer without browning for 1 minute. Remove from the heat and let stand for 5 minutes. Using a spoon, skim the foam off the surface of the melted butter.

2 Pour the melted butter into a glass bowl, leaving any white milk solids behind in the saucepan. Let cool to room temperature. Cover with plastic wrap and refrigerate until the butter is firm, at least 2 hours or up to overnight.

3 Remove the butter from the bowl. Wipe off any white milk solids that cling to the butter. Remelt the butter in a saucepan (or in a microwave), and pour into a clean bowl or covered container. Let cool. The clarified butter can be stored, covered, in the refrigerator, for up to 2 months. To use, remove as much as you need from the bowl, and remelt it.

MAKES ABOUT ⅔ CUP (5 FL OZ/160 ML)

PORTAGE BAY CAFE'S HOLLANDAISE SAUCE

4 large egg yolks

2 tablespoons fresh lemon juice

Kosher salt and freshly ground pepper

1 cup (8 oz/250 g) unsalted butter

1 In a blender, combine the egg yolks, lemon juice, ⅛ teaspoon salt, and a few grinds of pepper. In a saucepan, melt the butter over medium heat. With the blender running, slowly add the melted butter through the vent in the lid, processing until the sauce is thick. Taste and adjust the seasoning. If the sauce is too thick, add a little water to thin it.

2 Transfer the hollandaise sauce to a heatproof bowl. Cover and place over (not touching) a saucepan of hot, not simmering, water to keep warm.

variation For a less lemony sauce, use 1 tablespoon fresh lemon juice and add 1 tablespoon water.

MAKES ABOUT 1½ CUPS (12 FL OZ/375 ML)

HOMEMADE KETCHUP

1 can (28 oz/875 g) crushed plum tomatoes

¼ cup (2 1/2 oz/75 g) light corn syrup

3 tablespoons cider vinegar

2 tablespoons minced yellow onion

2 tablespoons red bell pepper

1 small clove garlic, minced

1 tablespoon firmly packed light brown sugar

Pinch of ground allspice

Pinch of ground cloves

Pinch of celery seeds

Pinch of yellow mustard seeds

½ bay leaf

Kosher salt and freshly ground pepper

1 At least 1 day before serving, in a heavy saucepan, combine the tomatoes, corn syrup, cider vinegar, onion, bell pepper, garlic, brown sugar, allspice, cloves, celery seeds, mustard seeds, ½ bay leaf, 1 teaspoon salt, and ⅛ teaspoon pepper. Bring to a boil over medium heat, stirring frequently. Reduce the heat to medium-low and cook at a brisk simmer, stirring frequently, until the mixture thickens and has reduced by half, about 1 hour.

2 Pass the mixture through a medium-mesh sieve into a heatproof bowl, discarding any solids that are left in the sieve. Let cool completely. Transfer to a covered container and refrigerate overnight to allow the flavors to blend before using. Use at once or cover and refrigerate for up to 2 weeks.

MAKES ABOUT 1½ CUPS (12 OZ/375 G)

PESTO

1 or 2 cloves garlic

¼ cup (1¼ oz/40 g) pine nuts

2 cups (2 oz/60 g) packed fresh basil leaves

½ cup (4 fl oz/125 ml) olive oil

½ cup (2 oz/60 g) freshly grated Parmesan cheese

Kosher salt and freshly ground pepper

1 With a food processor running, drop the garlic through the feed tube and process until minced. Turn off the processor, add the pine nuts, and pulse a few times to chop. Add the basil and pulse a few times to chop coarsely. Then, with the processor running, add the oil through the feed tube in a slow, steady steam and process until a smooth, moderately thick paste forms, stopping to scrape down the bowl as needed.

2 Transfer to a bowl and stir in the Parmesan. Season to taste with salt and pepper. Use at once, or transfer to a storage container, top with a thin layer of oil, cover tightly, and refrigerate for up to 1 week.

MAKES ABOUT 1 CUP (8 FL OZ/250 ML)

PICO DE GALLO

2 large ripe tomatoes, seeded and diced

½ cup (2½ oz/75 g) finely chopped yellow onion

3 tablespoons minced fresh cilantro

1 tablespoon fresh lime juice

½ jalapeño chile, seeded and minced, or more to taste

Kosher salt

1 In a nonreactive bowl, combine the tomatoes, onion, cilantro, lime juice, and jalapeño. Season with salt. Cover and let stand at room temperature for at least 30 minutes or up to 3 hours.

MAKES ABOUT 2½ CUPS (20 OZ/625 G)

CAFE PASQUAL'S GREEN CHILE SAUCE

2 lb (1 kg) fresh Anaheim chiles

4 tablespoons (2 fl oz/60 ml) canola oil

1 cup (4 oz/125 g) diced white onion

4 cloves garlic, minced

2 teaspoons dried marjoram

1 teaspoon ground cumin

3 tablespoons all-purpose flour

Kosher salt

1 Preheat the broiler. Arrange the chiles on a rimmed baking sheet and broil, turning occasionally, until blackened on all sides, about 12 minutes. Transfer the chiles to a bowl, cover tightly with plastic wrap, and let cool until easy to handle. Working with one chile at a time, peel off the blackened skin. Discard the stem, seeds, and ribs, and chop the chiles.

2 In a large, heavy saucepan, combine 1 quart (1 l) water with the chopped chiles and bring to a boil over high heat. Meanwhile, in a frying pan, warm 2 tablespoons of the oil over medium heat. Add the onion and cook until translucent, about 3 minutes. Stir in the garlic, marjoram, and cumin and cook until fragrant, about 1 minute. Add the onion mixture to the saucepan with the chiles, reduce the heat to medium-low, and simmer, stirring occasionally, until the chiles are very tender and the cooking liquid is cloudy, about 20 minutes.

3 In a medium saucepan, warm the remaining 2 tablespoons oil over low heat. Add the flour all at once and cook, whisking constantly, until the mixture is dark beige with a nutty aroma, about 3 minutes. Whisk in about 1½ cups (12 fl oz/375 ml) of the chile mixture, then return to the larger saucepan. Return to a simmer. Cook, stirring often, until no trace of raw flour flavor remains, about 15 minutes. Season to taste with salt. If desired, working in batches, in a blender, process the chile mixture until smooth. The sauce can be cooled, covered, and refrigerated for up to 4 days or frozen for up to 2 months.

MAKES ABOUT 4½ CUPS (36 FL OZ/1.1 L)

CAFE PASQUAL'S RED CHILE SAUCE

16 guajillo chiles, stemmed, seeded, and halved

8 ancho chiles, stemmed, seeded, and halved

4 dried chiles de arbol, stemmed and seeded

1 cup (4 oz/125 g) coarsely chopped white onion

2 cloves garlic

1 tablespoon red wine vinegar

1 teaspoon dried oregano, preferably Mexican

Kosher salt

1 Bring 1 quart (1 l) water to a boil over high heat. Add the chiles, onion, garlic, vinegar, oregano, and 1 tablespoon salt. Return to a boil and cook until the chiles soften, about 5 minutes. Remove from the heat and let cool completely.

2 Working in batches, in a blender, process the chile mixture until smooth. With a wooden spoon, pass the sauce through a coarse-mesh wire sieve to remove any tough chile skins.

MAKES ABOUT 4 CUPS (32 FL OZ/1 L)

REFRIED BEANS

2 tablespoons olive oil

3 thick slices applewood-smoked bacon, coarsely chopped

1 small yellow onion, finely chopped

1 jalapeño chile, seeded and minced

1 garlic clove, minced

½ teaspoon ground cumin

2 cans (15 oz/470 g each) pinto beans

Kosher salt

1 In a large, heavy frying pan, preferably cast iron, heat the oil over medium heat. Add the bacon and cook, stirring frequently, until crisp and golden, about 6 minutes. Using a slotted spoon, transfer the bacon to paper towels to drain, leaving the fat in the pan.

2 Add the onion, jalapeño, and garlic to the fat in the pan and reduce the heat to medium. Cook, stirring occasionally, until the onion is translucent and the garlic is fragrant, 3–4 minutes. Stir in the cumin.

3 Drain the beans, but reserve the liquid. Add the beans, ½ cup (3½ oz/105 g) at a time, to the frying pan, mashing them into a rough paste with a wooden spoon. When all of the beans have been mashed, stir in enough of the reserved cooking liquid until the beans have the desired texture. Stir in the bacon, then season to taste with salt. Serve hot.

MAKES 4–6 SERVINGS

CHICKEN STOCK

1 whole chicken, about 4 lb (2 kg)

1 yellow onion, coarsely chopped

1 large carrot, coarsely chopped

1 large stalk celery, coarsely chopped

4 sprigs fresh flat-leaf parsley

4 sprigs fresh thyme, or ½ teaspoon dried thyme

¼ teaspoon black peppercorns

1 bay leaf

1 Using a large, sharp knife, cut the chicken into 2 wings, 2 breast halves, 2 drumsticks, 2 thighs, and the back. Reserve the heart, gizzard, kidneys, and liver for another use.

2 In a stockpot, combine the cut-up chicken, onion, carrot, celery, and cold water to cover by 1 inch (2.5 cm). Raise the heat to high and bring to a boil, skimming off any foam that rises to the surface. Add the parsley, thyme, peppercorns, and bay leaf, reduce the heat to low, and simmer gently, uncovered, until the chicken breasts show no sign of pink when pierced with a knife in the thickest part, about 45 minutes.

3 Remove the breasts from the pot, leaving the rest of the parts simmering in the stock. Remove the skin and bones and return them to the pot. Set the breast meat aside. Continue simmering the stock until full-flavored, about 30 minutes more.

4 Remove the stock from the heat and strain through a colander set over a large heatproof bowl. Remove the thighs and drumsticks from the colander. Discard their skin and bones along with the solids in the colander. Add the meat from the drumsticks and thighs to the reserved breast meat. Let the meat cool, cover, and refrigerate for another use. Let the stock stand for 5 minutes, then skim off the fat from the surface. Use at once, or let cool, cover, and refrigerate for up to 3 days or freeze for up to 3 months.

MAKES ABOUT 2 QUARTS (2 L)

QUICK PUFF PASTRY

2 cups (1 lb/500 g) unsalted butter

2 cups (10 oz/315 g) unbleached flour

²/₃ cup (3 oz/90 g) cake flour

1 teaspoon fine sea salt

1 cup (8 fl oz/250 ml) ice water

1 Cut the butter into ½-inch (12-mm) cubes and spread on a baking sheet. Freeze for 30 minutes.

2 In the bowl of a stand mixer, combine the unbleached flour, cake flour, and salt. Add the chilled butter and toss to coat with the flour mixture. Place the bowl on the mixer and fit with the paddle attachment. Mix on low speed until the butter cubes are about half their original size, 1-1½ minutes. Add the ice water and mix just until the dough comes together into a very moist mass.

3 Turn the dough out onto a floured work surface and pat into a rectangle. Dust the top of the dough well with flour. Roll out into a 16-by-8-inch (40-by-20-cm) rectangle, with the short side facing you. Using a pastry brush, gently brush off the excess flour from the surface of the dough. Fold the bottom third of the dough up, then fold the top third of the

dough down over it, as if folding a letter. Rotate the dough a quarter turn, with the folded side to your left, and repeat the process again, rolling the dough into a 16-by-8-inch (40-by-20-cm) rectangle, and folding it into thirds. Turn again and repeat the rolling and folding a third and fourth time, being sure to brush off the excess flour before folding. Wrap in plastic wrap and refrigerate for at least 30 minutes or up to 2 hours.

4 Roll and fold the dough twice more. Rewrap in plastic wrap and refrigerate for at least 30 minutes or up to 2 hours. Place the dough on the work surface, again with the short side facing you. Using a large, sharp knife, with a single push without rocking the knife back and forth, cut the dough in half horizontally.

5 Wrap each dough half in plastic wrap and refrigerate for at least 1 hour or up to 2 days before using. (The dough can be frozen, overwrapped with aluminum foil, for up to 2 months. Defrost it overnight in the refrigerator. If the dough is still very hard, let it stand at room temperature for about 10 minutes. Then pound the dough, vertically and horizontally, with the rolling pin until it is pliable but still cold.)

MAKES ABOUT 2½ LB (1.25 KG)

BUTTERY PASTRY DOUGH

1¼ cups (6½ oz/200 g) all-purpose flour

¼ teaspoon fine sea salt

7 tablespoons (3½ oz/105 g) unsalted butter, chilled

¼ cup (2 fl oz/60 ml) ice water, or as needed

1 In a large bowl, whisk together the flour and salt. Cut the butter into cubes and scatter over the flour mixture. Using a pastry blender or 2 knives, cut the butter into the flour mixture just until the mixture forms coarse crumbs about the size of peas.

2 Drizzle the ice water over the flour mixture and toss with a fork until the mixture forms moist clumps.

If the dough seems too crumbly, add a little more ice water.

3 Form the dough into a disk (some flakes of butter should be visible), wrap in plastic wrap, and refrigerate for at least 30 minutes or up to 2 hours. Or, overwrap with aluminum foil and freeze for up to 1 month, then thaw in the refrigerator before using.

MAKES ENOUGH FOR ONE 9-INCH (23-CM) QUICHE OR TART

SWEET YEAST DOUGH

1 cup (8 fl oz/250 ml) whole milk

1/2 cup (4 oz/125 g) granulated sugar

5 tablespoons (21/2 oz/75 g) unsalted butter, melted and cooled

3 large eggs

1 package (21/2 teaspoons) quick-rise yeast

5 cups (25 oz/780 g) unbleached all-purpose flour, as needed

11/4 teaspoons fine sea salt

1 In the bowl of a stand mixer, combine the milk, sugar, butter, eggs, and yeast. Add 41/2 cups (221/2 oz/705 g) of the flour and the salt. Place the bowl on the mixer and fit with the paddle attachment. Mix on medium-low speed, adding as much of the remaining flour as needed to make a soft dough that does not stick to the bowl.

2 Replace the paddle attachment with the dough hook. Knead the dough on medium-low speed, adding more flour if needed, until it is smooth but still soft, 6–7 minutes. Shape the dough into a ball.

3 Butter a large bowl. Add the dough and turn to coat with the butter. Cover tightly with plastic wrap. Let the dough rise in a warm spot until it doubles in bulk, 11/2–2 hours. Use at once. Or, punch down the dough, cover tightly with plastic wrap, and refrigerate for up to 12 hours. Punch down the dough and let stand at room temperature for 1 hour before using.

MAKES ABOUT 21/4 LB (34 OZ/1.1 KG)

SWEETENED WHIPPED CREAM

1 cup (8 fl oz/250 ml) heavy cream

2 tablespoons sugar

1/2 teaspoon pure vanilla extract

1 In a chilled bowl, combine the cream, sugar, and vanilla. Using a handheld mixer on medium-high speed, beat until soft peaks form. Use at once or cover and refrigerate for up to 2 hours before serving.

MAKES ABOUT 2 CUPS (16 FL OZ/500 ML)

CHOCOLATE ICING

3/4 cup (6 fl oz/180 ml) heavy cream

6 oz (185 g) semisweet chocolate, finely chopped

1 tablespoon unsalted butter, cut into small pieces

1 tablespoon light corn syrup

1 In a small saucepan, bring the cream to a simmer over medium heat. Put the chocolate, butter, and corn syrup in a small bowl. Pour the hot cream into the bowl and let stand to soften the chocolate, about 3 minutes. Whisk until the chocolate is melted. Let stand 5 minutes to cool slightly.

MAKES ABOUT 11/2 CUPS (12 FL OZ/375 ML)

LEMON ICING

2 cups (8 oz/250 g) confectioners' sugar

Finely grated zest of 1 lemon, preferably Meyer

2 tablespoons fresh lemon juice, preferably Meyer

1 Sift the confectioners' sugar into a small bowl. Add the lemon zest and juice. Whisk in up to 3 tablespoons water, as needed, to make a glaze that is just thicker than heavy cream.

MAKES ABOUT 3/4 CUP (6 FL OZ/180 ML)

BASIC TECHNIQUES

TOASTING NUTS AND SEEDS

1 Be sure to toast nuts and seeds just before you are ready to use them. Preheat the oven to 350°F (180°C).

2 Spread the nuts or seeds in a single layer on a small rimmed baking sheet and toast, stirring occasionally, until fragrant, 2–10 minutes for seeds and 5–15 minutes for nuts. The timing will vary depending on the type or size; check regularly to avoid burning.

SKINNING HAZELNUTS

Toast the hazelnuts as directed above, removing them from the oven when they are fragrant and their skins have cracked. Pour the still-warm nuts into a coarse-textured kitchen towel and rub vigorously to remove the skins. Don't worry if tiny bits of skin remain.

MAKING FRESH BREAD CRUMBS

1 Start with slices of slightly stale bread with a sturdy texture (use bread about 2 days past its peak of freshness, or lay fresh bread slices flat on a sheet pan overnight to dry out).

2 Tear the bread into small pieces and drop into the work bowl of a food processor. Pulse until the pieces are chopped into small crumbs.

ZESTING CITRUS

The best tool for zesting citrus is a fine-rasp Microplane grater. Hold the fruit in the palm of one hand over a bowl and pull the grater across the fruit with the other hand, following the contour of the fruit and removing only the colored portion of the rind, and not the white pith.

Tap the grater firmly on the side of the bowl to release the zest. If you don't have a Microplane or other fine-rasp grater, remove the zest with a vegetable peeler (take care not to include the bitter white pith) and then finely mince the zest with a sharp knife.

ROASTING BELL PEPPERS

1 Preheat the broiler. Place the bell pepper(s) on a baking sheet and broil, turning occasionally, until blackened on all sides, about 12 minutes. Transfer to a cutting board and let cool until easy to handle.

2 Peel off the blackened skin from the pepper(s). Remove and discard the stem, seeds, and ribs, then slice or chop the pepper(s) as directed.

SEEDING AND MINCING CHILES

1 Many cooks wear a disposable latex glove when working with chiles to prevent skin irritation. Using a paring knife, cut the chile into halves lengthwise, then into quarters.

2 Cut away the seeds and ribs from each chile quarter, if desired (this will lessen the heat of the chile). Cut the quarters lengthwise into narrow strips, then cut the strips crosswise to mince them.

CUTTING CORN OFF THE COB

Stand the ear of corn, wide end down, upright in a shallow bowl and, using a chef's knife, slice down between the kernels and the cob, rotating the ear one-quarter turn after each cut and capturing the kernels in the bowl.

INDEX

weldon**owen**

415 Jackson Street, Suite 200, San Francisco, CA 94111
Telephone: 415 291 0100 Fax: 415 291 8841
www.weldonowen.com

A division of

BONNIER

BREAKFAST COMFORTS
Conceived and produced by Weldon Owen, Inc.
in collaboration with Williams-Sonoma, Inc.
3250 Van Ness Avenue, San Francisco, CA 94109

Printed and bound in China by 1010 Printing, Ltd.
This edition first printed in 2013
10 9 8 7 6 5 4 3 2 1

Library of Congress Cataloging-in-Publication data is available

ISBN-13: 978-1-61628-601-9
ISBN-10: 1-61628-601-6

A WELDON OWEN PRODUCTION
First edition copyright © 2010 Weldon Owen, Inc.
and Williams-Sonoma, Inc.

This edition copyright © 2013

All rights reserved, including the right of reproduction
in whole or in part in any form.

Photographer Maren Caruso
Food Stylist Robyn Valarik
Prop Stylist Leigh Noe

ACKNOWLEDGMENTS
Weldon Owen wishes to thank the following people for their generous support in producing this book: .
David Evans, Leslie Evans, Rachel Lopez Metzger, Deneane Niebergall, Elizabeth Parson, Emily Polar, Elise Ravet,
Lesli Sommerdorf, Jane Tunks, Stacy Ventura, Jason Wheeler, and Tracy White.

Weldon Owen and Rick Rodgers would like to extend their gratitude
to the owners and workers of the restaurants who participated in this project:
Blu Jam Cafe, Cafe Pasqual's, Daily Cafe, Hell's Kitchen, Highland Bakery, Hominy Grill,
HotChocolate, Jack's Firehouse, Kerbey Lane Cafe, Michael's Genuine Food & Drink, Portage Bay Cafe,
The Ruby Slipper Cafe, Sarabeth's, Snooze Eatery, Sweet 16th - A Bakery, and Universal Cafe.

All photographs by Maren Caruso except for the following:
Davis Ayer (page 53, bottom); Sabina Bonvillain (page 63, top); Emma Boys (page 40, bottom);
David Burch (page 7, bottom left and bottom right; page 20, bottom); John Casado (page 7, middle; page 147, top);
June Cochran (page 162, top); Brian Doben (back flap); Peter Frank Edwards (page 7, top left and top right; page 193, top; back cover, middle left);
Mick Houston (page 7, middle left; page 76, bottom); Kristi Kienholz (page 117, top); Alan Klehr (page 128, bottom);
Kitty Leaken (page 181, bottom); Mark J. Logan (page 171, bottom); Melissa Madison Fuller (page 154, bottom); Kristina Sacci (page 30, top);
Jackie Sayet (page 7, middle right; page 104, bottom); Tucker + Hossler (page 204); Ben Yap (page 86, top).

Front cover: Raised Belgian Waffles with Strawberries and Whipped Cream.
Back cover: Monkey Bread with Strawberry Caramel Sauce; Maple-Glazed Bacon with Cracked Black Pepper;
Sweet Potato Pancakes with Pecans and Brown-Sugar Sauce; Cinnamon Rolls with Cream Cheese Icing.